Our True Nature

From *Awakening* to *Understanding*

DANIEL KAST

BALBOA.PRESS

A DIVISION OF HAY HOUSE

Balboa Press books may be ordered through booksellers or by contacting:

Balboa Press
A Division of Hay House
1663 Liberty Drive
Bloomington, IN 47403
www.balboapress.com
844-682-1282

Cover Art by Yelana Elefante

Print information available on the last page.

ISBN: 978-1-9822-6813-8 (sc)
ISBN: 978-1-9822-6815-2 (hc)
ISBN: 978-1-9822-6814-5 (e)

Library of Congress Control Number: 2021908469

Balboa Press rev. date: 04/26/2021

Dedication

I wish to dedicate this book first to my family, who unknowingly has been the inspiration for much of it. To Kaia, Paul, Adam, Michael, Danielle, Dean, and Denise, with whom I shared some of my early writings. Your feedback, support, and encouragement have given me the courage and conviction to write this book. To Chris, who taught me to pour my heart and myself into the book, to give it passion and personality. To Dominick, for teaching me how to sit and observe, and for helping me clear away much of the wreckage of my past, which was preventing me from growing and from enjoying my present. To Debbie, for her love, her light, and her spiritual guidance and inspiration. To Michael Singer, Eckhart Tolle, Thich Nhat Hanh, Ram Dass, Sri Nisargadatta Maharaj, and all of those whose works I have read that have helped me find my way home to my true Self. They have inspired the writing of this book. And to the countless others, who have loved me, supported me, nurtured me, taught me, encouraged me, and helped me heal. For all of you, I will be forever grateful. A heartfelt Thank You to all.

Contents

Introduction

So, you have found my book. Whether it was recommended to you by a friend or you simply stumbled across it by chance, here we are. Since I have your attention, please allow me first to say thank you, then to take the opportunity to give you a little background about me and my life as well as about this book.

Presently, I have spent the last forty-eight years living and experiencing a human existence. The first eighteen years was a purely physical experience. I had no concept of the spirit, soul, or anything aside from the physical world. My parents were from two different religious backgrounds. Neither of them, however, practiced their religion. As a result, my sisters and I were left to figure out for ourselves what we believed in and what worked for us. While I appreciated the freedom we were given, I probably could have used a little more direction, for I wound up believing in nothing. I thought that anyone who believed in any type of deity was abnormal or unhealthy. I had imaginary friends as a child, as do many children, but as I grew up I outgrew them. I assumed that those who believed in such things never did. In any case, during this purely physical stage of my experience, many of the activities I engaged in were reckless and dangerous because they gave me that rush mix of fear and excitement that enabled me to feel something besides empty. You see, as a young child I was highly sensitive, intuitive, and emotional but I was surrounded by a family of nearly stoic people. It was not that they were evil or wicked, or that they did not care, but their ability to express emotion and to show love seemed almost nonexistent. This perceived emotional neglect left me feeling completely abandoned, alienated, and alone. I remember always having a deep feeling that something was not quite right with the world. I felt that things were somehow supposed to be different from how they were. At the time, though, I was too young to understand or to articulate what I felt. I felt that I had no one to go to, no one to ask questions of, nor anyone to express my feelings to. It seemed as if I were vastly different from everyone else. As a result, I came to think that perhaps I was the "something" that was wrong. I learned to bury these feelings, eventually reaching a point where I felt empty, completely devoid of emotion and love. I did this just so that I could try to fit in and be like others. Emptiness became my constant companion. I was too young to realize how damaging this was. I did not learn until later, during my spiritual journey, that I had inadvertently cut myself off from my spirit, from my true self. This self-severance left me, in essence, only half a person, only a frail image or a crude representation of who I truly was. To live only a half-life, only a physical life, left me feeling as if I were dying inside. That pain, however, became the catalyst for change. It launched me on the thirty-year spiritual journey that I am still on today. I've come to understand that the part of me that always felt that way, the part of me that I tried to bury, was my true Self. It had been crying out to me, trying to get my attention, trying to claw its way back to the surface so that I could see the truth. It had survived no matter how much adrenaline-fueled running, avoiding, and burying I did. It eventually screamed out and demanded to be acknowledged and heard. That forced me to seek out help and to seek answers. I will not go into too much detail here, because I will share much of this throughout the book. What I will share here is that I came to know my true Self. I learned of my spirit and the spiritual realm. What I found and learned eventually filled the emptiness in me, healed me, and enabled me to feel whole again. It has left me feeling alive, energetic, and full of compassion and love. It has been the inspiration for most of the writing that has transpired. It has given me the motivation and the courage to finally assemble this book.

Although throughout my journey I have explored many religions and spiritual teachings, I do not follow any one specific discipline. Rather, I have taken bits and pieces from various sources along the way and have developed habits, rituals, routines, and beliefs that work for me. Early on in my journey, I read Herman Hesse's *Siddhartha*. It touched me deeply. The idea of finding my own way, of carving my own path, appealed greatly to me. Although it has been a long, challenging, and often painful road, I don't believe I could have arrived here any other way. I might consider myself awakened or enlightened, but by no means do I consider myself an expert, guru, or spiritual teacher. In fact, many years of this journey have been spent unchecked, wallowing in old, useless, dysfunctional patterns of behavior that served only to cause me suffering. However, it was that suffering that brought about the need and desire for change so I embrace and honor it. As Eckhart Tolle says, "Suffering is only necessary until you realize it is unnecessary." I do believe, though, that we are all capable of being teachers as well as students. While we are all sharing this human experience, hopefully learning, growing, and evolving along the way (as students), we also possess (as teachers) knowledge, wisdom, and experience that could benefit others. To that end, this book is a collection of essays that originally chronicled my first year of awakening: the awe followed by the wonder, the light of pure awareness followed by the light of realization and understanding. It is still that for the most part, but there have been revisions that reflect the deeper understanding that has evolved over the past three years since that awakening. I believe I have preserved most of the original content, thereby retaining the book's natural arc and flow, but with improved articulation and clarity. It is as much a journal as it is a source of information. Each chapter contains within it a realization I have had along the way. All that is written has arrived through inspiration alone, either directly out of meditation or upon awakening, before the mind could have a hand in it. I have also included quite a bit of personal experience that I believe makes this information tangible. Such experience gives it roots in reality, in actual practice rather than simply remaining abstract ideas. Hopefully, it is relatable as well as informative.

If you are one of those who have awakened, I hope this book fills you with yups, uh-huhs, head nods of identification, and the realization that you are not alone. If not, then this book might not offer much to you. But maybe, just maybe, something in these pages can crack open your eyes, your mind, and your heart enough to see, enough to catch a glimpse of what awaits you on the other side of awakening. I encourage you to join me on the amazing journey I have had these past few years and throughout life. It is an honor and a privilege to have the opportunity to share it with you.

Transformation

At their very best, words rarely wed well with a transformative spiritual experience. The two are not of the same world. Such experiences leave one awestruck and speechless. It is with words, though, that one wonders about and conveys to others that sense of awe. Therefore, herein I use words in my attempt to convey the events that took place the night of my transformation. Looking back, I can see clearly the chain of events that led to that night. That night, however, was something to behold unto itself. It demands telling. To remain silent would be a disservice.

Sunday had come and gone. Monday morning, just past midnight, as usual, I was puttering around on social media before heading to bed. I came upon a philosophical question a friend had posted and was looking for responses to. I generally don't engage in such discussions, particularly on social media. I consider my beliefs and philosophies to be my own, just as you may feel that yours are your own. I'm content to simply let them be. It was an interesting question though, so as I read through the list of responses, I felt compelled to share my thoughts. Because such communication is deeply personal, I responded in a private message. I didn't want to subject it or myself to the scrutiny and possible misunderstandings or misinterpretations of a public forum. What ensued was a long, detailed, profound response that flowed not from my mind but from somewhere deep inside me, from an intelligence far beyond what my mind was capable of on its own. It was as if something had been stirred and awakened in me as if a flood gate had opened and my response was the subsequent deluge. So much so that, upon re-reading the response I had written, I had to step back and sort of scratch my head and wonder where it all came from.

I decided to meditate on it. I had been practicing meditation for some time, with only marginal success. I had gotten to the point where I could pretty effectively quiet my mind and experience some stillness and peace, but little else. Even accomplishing that had taken a few years and a tremendous amount of diligence. This night, though, was to be transformative. As I settled in, allowing my mind to settle as well, a profound sense of calm and stillness came over me. I had not known such a state before, and I fell into a deeper meditation than I ever had. My body vanished. It was not as though I had been projected out of it, but fell deep inside, beneath it almost, like a trap door had opened and I had slipped through. Though I was still me, I was not limited to the confines of my physical form. I was pure consciousness: formless, life energy, and I had discovered a new dimension, an entire universe within. As I began to observe my surroundings, I noticed all around me a seemingly infinite number of other energies as shapeless as I was. All of us streamed within a current of energy, a tether if you will, leading to a Source from which all such energies seemed to emanate and return to simultaneously. As I followed my tether, drifting towards and into that Source, I felt completely embraced, completely bathed in light and warmth, enveloped in love, as a newborn being held by its mother. I felt as if I was being cleansed, as if every bit of negativity, every fear, every doubt, and every insecurity was being washed away. It was as if I had merged with or become one with that Source. I realized that each of the energies I observed was the consciousness of every other being in existence and that we all stem from and are connected to that same Source. That we are, in essence, the same being, all branches of The Tree of Life. I could feel every being as one single entity. Every thought, every emotion, every event, every experience, as well as every scrap of knowledge or information that had ever existed or will ever exist I witnessed simultaneously as a singular experience. I was witnessing all of existence without the limitations of time or space. I had been given a glimpse of what it is like to be that Source. Yet, because I had never felt or experienced anything even beginning to approach this, because it was so unfamiliar, it was almost indescribably overwhelming and far beyond my comprehension. I could not grasp what I was experiencing. I could only be there to witness it. After what could have been a split second, or an eternity (timelessness tends to have that effect), I drifted back into my body and slowly arose. An hour had gone by, but it felt as if an eternity had been lived in a single moment. At the time I could not explain how or why, but I knew I was different. That profound sense of calmness and peace was still with me. The never-ending stream of thoughts that was usually in my head was no more. I felt no fear, doubt, nor worry. I knew that none of the insecurities I had previously felt were real, that they had been constructed by my mind. I felt almost nothing that reminded me of who I had been before this experience. I was changed, transformed. Into what, I was still unsure. I was still trying to wrap my head around the experience I just had. I knew it was something I would never fully comprehend, for it was an experience of the spirit, not of the mind. It was something that I *knew* from my core required no thought, no explanation, no categorizing, or labeling, as our minds love to do. I knew I would never go back to who I had been. I knew I couldn't. There was no way back. Why would I even want to? Why would I ever want to go back to that person who was ravaged by his mind, plagued with fear and doubt, and subject to a never-ending barrage of negative thoughts and feelings? That was not who I was anymore. Since then, whenever my mind would try to stir up those afflictive emotions in me, drawing me in and away from the present moment, those feelings would be fleeting and have no real power over me anymore. I don't want to minimize or understate this though. The old behavior and mind patterns carry with them a habitual nature and a momentum from years of use. Diligence and discipline are required to stay removed from them. But knowing that I had a way out now, a way to escape the confines and trappings of my mind, I knew they would be short-lived. I knew that there was much more than just this physical realm, that it was minuscule when compared to the spiritual. I knew I was much more than just my body, that consciousness, which inhabits my body, extends way beyond its physical confines. In actuality, the body exists in consciousness, in that spiritual realm. I discovered that the entire physical dimension is manifested in that spiritual realm, in that vast universe beyond form. I knew that I could go there any time but didn't need to "go" anywhere because it was not a place to "go" that was separate from me, but a place to "be" that I could abide within myself, repose within myself. I knew that I could do so at any moment, simply by becoming still and bringing my attention inside and away from my mind and the outer world.

Resuming my life after this experience, I can only describe myself as having been born again. Every experience, even seemingly mundane, everyday tasks are fresh, new, and exciting as if it's the first time I'm experiencing them. Life has lost its seriousness (or perhaps I have). Life is fun, playful, and full of joy and wonder. Responsibilities that used to weigh so heavily on me seem to have lost their significance. They're now more like games to me, games to be played out but not taken too seriously. My relationships with others and interactions with people are warm, friendly, caring, and loving. The defensive walls I had built between myself and others have all but melted away, and I feel a real connection with everyone and everything around me. I often find myself struck with spontaneous smiles and laughter, for no other reason than the joy I feel. Sometimes that feeling is so intense that I shed tears of gratitude. I have a tremendous feeling of love in my heart, an almost burning flame that is constantly alive and flowing out into the world. It affects everyone I come in contact with. Friends and coworkers have asked me what's going on, that I seem different. They've asked me what has changed. To most, I tend to shy away from the subject, simply offering a basic explanation that the average person can accept. I will say, "I'm having a good day" or "I'm in a good place." To the few who I feel can understand the experience I had and who are sharing this spiritual journey with me, I've related the details of my experience to them as best as I can. As mentioned in the beginning, words cannot adequately convey the awe of a spiritual experience, but I attempt to do so because I want to share with them the love and light that I feel. I also seem to have a sense of knowing and understanding of things that there is no logical reason for me to be able to know or understand. Information that I have not learned nor been taught. Yet, when the need arises, the information just seems to be there. I don't mean I suddenly know how to fly a plane or that I can perform brain surgery. I mean, simply, that I comprehend things of a more spiritual nature. Things such as how the body and mind are meant to be instruments, not an identity, what love is, my connection to it, as well as the relationship between the body, mind, consciousness, and the world. I understand the behavior of others and can distinguish between their behavior and who they truly are. I sense the connectedness of all things. All this happens through the connection to the Source. I believe this information is being drawn from the well of knowledge that I briefly tapped into during my experience and is now being granted to me on an "as-needed" basis, so as not to overwhelm me. My friend calls these "celestial downloads." Mostly the information is pulled directly out of meditation or out of sleep, upon awakening, before my mind has a chance to activate. I have also had the experience of perceiving events without time. A flash in my mind of something happening shortly before it happens. I'm not referring to common circumstances that can be anticipated based on history or routine or cycles. I'm referring to out-of-the-ordinary circumstances that stand out, but that I've seen before they happen. I'm not a fortune teller, nor do

I believe I can see the future. However, this has happened far too many times to be a mere coincidence. Again, these moments are a reminder that my connection to the Source still exists. I believe these glimpses, as well as the ability to access previously unknown information, serve as proof, as evidence that the experience I had was real and not some fantasy or delusion created by my mind. This experience was something far beyond what my mind is capable of conceiving or comprehending on its own. It was a true spiritual experience: an awakening, enlightenment, a transformation. Whatever words I choose to use to describe it, it was a monumental and deeply meaningful experience that has left me awestruck, deeply humbled, and overwhelmed with gratitude. It has changed me and has changed the course of my life. It demanded telling because everything going forward has been the result of and inspired by this experience.

Human-Being

Have you ever wondered why we are called *human beings*? It is because we are made up of two parts. The first component is the "human," our physical form, our designation as a species. The second component is the non-physical aspect, our "being" which is comprised of our consciousness and life force. Consciousness is often referred to as *spirit, soul, atman,* or *inner self,* whereas the life force can be called *energy, chi,* or *prana.* Whichever names you choose, this "being" is the very *essence* of who we are. The words are not nearly as important as our realization and acknowledgment of both components. In truth, they are two sides of the same coin, two halves of the whole. The connection and harmony between these two parts are what makes us complete.

We live in a physical world, and our current existence is form-based. Because of this, much of our focus and attention is given to form: our bodies, our thoughts, our feelings, our beliefs, things outside us, other people, situations, events, and so on. This constant attention on the physical ultimately results in the loss of connection with our "being", our formless essence. As we grow, we are taught to speak, to feed ourselves, to bathe, to dress, to read, to write, to interact with others, to exist in this world and everything that goes along with it. Rarely, however, are we taught to be still, to bring our focus into the present moment where our essence can be felt, to bring our attention to our "being", to the other part of who we are. This type of conditioning is the main reason we suffer this loss of connection. If our families live in such a disconnected state, we learn to live that way as well. I spent most of my childhood and adolescence in such a state: disconnected from "being" and aware only of the physical.

The denial of or loss of connection to this part of us is what causes the feeling that there is a "hole" in us, a vacuity. This emptiness is what causes us to feel incomplete: that we are, somehow, not enough. Also, the physical reality that much of our attention is on is transient. It is ever-changing and temporary. That impermanence, that lack of stability and constancy, is the void from where our fear and all its psychological and physical manifestations arise. Worry, doubt, insecurity, uncertainty, anxiety, depression, unhappiness, negativity, restlessness, anger, hostility, violence, seeing others and the world as a threat—all stem from this instability. The impermanence of our physical reality seems to threaten our very existence. When we are focused only on the physical part of who we are, the perpetual stress of this feeling of impermanence causes us to often feel fatigued and tired, even after a full night's sleep. That type of constantly perceived threat is draining. It wears us out. Our longings for stability, security, safety, wholeness, and completeness can never be achieved through focusing only on the physical. We can temporarily satisfy such longings through outside things, but that satisfaction proves to be nothing but fleeting. It never lasts, and the feeling of emptiness always returns.

What I have learned is that we need to re-acquaint ourselves with our essence, which inhabits our body yet is so much greater than it. We need to be able to pay attention to both aspects of who we are. Doing so fills in the gaps. The stability and constancy that this physical world lacks can be found in the spiritual dimension deep within, where our "being" resides. It can only be felt or experienced in the present moment. The now is timeless, meaning past and future exist only as fabrications of the mind. They are only thoughts: memories of what was and anticipation or projection of what is yet to come. The moment contains the very things our minds cannot find in the physical world: permanence, stability, and constancy. By bringing our attention to the now, to the present moment, we can reconnect with our essence, with our "being," and thus become complete again—whole. That emptiness or lack of completeness, that "hole" we feel becomes filled by that essence. Fear and all its manifestations simply melt away when both halves are connected, when we are complete.

Much to my dismay and frustration, I have also learned that these fear-based manifestations tend to linger in our minds because our minds can only perceive form. Our minds cannot grasp "being" because "being" cannot be thought, labeled, or categorized, it can only be experienced: through quietness, through the absence of thought. Therefore, the mind can never feel whole. The fear lingers in the background, in the unconscious, and sometimes becomes stirred up in us when something or someone triggers it and our attention is pulled into the mind and away from the present moment. The person, event, or situation outside of us or the thought or feeling inside of us that triggered the fear is not entirely irrelevant. After all, it is important to understand what causes such reactions. However, once our attention has been diverted from the moment and into our thoughts, we have lost the connection to our "being" and are then perceiving only through the fragile, impermanent, incomplete part of ourselves. Resolution cannot be found until we are once again whole. Fortunately, all we need to do to regain that wholeness is realize what has happened inside. The realization that our attention has been pulled away from the present moment and into the mind is all we need to pull our attention back into the moment, reconnecting both parts, once again re-establishing that wholeness. By becoming aware that we are not our thoughts, by seeing them objectively, we can separate our attention from our thoughts and our minds. We can then bring our attention back to the constancy and stability of the moment, to our "being", once again dispelling fear and freeing ourselves.

Especially since my awakening experience, I have found meditation to be a wonderful tool for accomplishing this. The sense of stillness and centeredness that unfolds during meditation creates the perfect environment to break away from the mind and its thoughts. Meditation does not have to be a huge undertaking. However long it takes to settle into stillness, to separate our attention from our thoughts, to bring our attention into the present and connect with our being, is all the time that is required. A few moments of conscious breathing are sometimes all we need to accomplish this. As with any new skill we learn, we become more proficient through practice. I'd like to suggest picturing the never-ending stream of thoughts as an actual stream. Indeed, it can be fun to play in at times, but it is impossible to be still in. The current pulls and pushes us and will drain us of all of our energy. It will tire us out if we remain aswim in it for too long. We simply need to decide to step out of the stream, to separate ourselves from it. In other words, we become aware of our thoughts objectively and decide to remove our attention from them. Once this is accomplished, awareness remains *as* our essence, our "being". Reunited with our essence, we are whole again, a "human-being" once more.

The Hug

We all know what a hug is: an embrace between individuals as an expression of love, caring, compassion, joy. This awakening, though, has transformed my understanding of a hug and has given it such a deeper meaning. A hug's reality is far greater than just this simple definition. It means so much more.

In the physical sense, a hug combines two into one. Its warm sense of union dissolves the sense of separation between us as two individuals. A hug temporarily connects us and makes us one being. There emerges a sense of love, warmth, and comfort from it. Beneath the surface waves of an embrace lies an ocean of sharing, a comingling and combining of energies, a union of spirits. As we embrace, we touch each other's hearts and realize that we are one: two streams of energy from the same source, two branches of the same tree of life. We realize that the separation between us is only physical, that we are all connected on a deeper spiritual level, and that, for the duration of the embrace, even the physical separation no longer exists.

The embrace, however, is only one-half of the experience. There is the letting go, the release of one another. The release is what gives the embrace its shape, its definition. The release gives the hug an end. It also gives the embrace significance, meaning, and value. It makes the embrace something to cherish and deeply appreciate. The release is just as important as the embrace. One simply cannot exist without the other. Letting go also teaches us a most valuable lesson. It teaches us of the impermanence of this world: that everything that exists in it, everything we know, even the world itself will eventually come to an end. Though this may seem like a sad fact, it is impermanence that gives our lives the same definition, meaning, and value. Impermanence helps us to cherish and appreciate what we have.

We do not leave the hug empty-handed, though. We each receive a parting gift. The combined energies of the hug create something new: a shared experience we get to take with us as a memory. We carry this memory with us and can recall it at any time to once again experience the love and warmth of the embrace as well as the letting go, reminding us to appreciate what we have, and to cherish the moments we have shared. Please, if you are reading this and know me personally, the next time we meet, share a hug with me so that I may add it to the collection. If we do not know each other personally, share a hug with someone you care about so you can enrich their lives as well as your own.

A Four-Letter Word
Called Love

Ah, love: one of the most overused, misused, and misunderstood words in our language. The word is often tossed around nonchalantly, devaluing both the word and the reality because of a lack of understanding of their depth and meaning. Love—the word and the reality— is also sometimes wielded as a weapon or tool to manipulate, confuse, or coerce. I know this firsthand because my misunderstanding and misuse of love have caused me to break hearts and hurt people. Thankfully though, as a result of this awakening, I also know that love is often expressed as the powerful, driving, healing force that it is. It has been the motivation behind countless poems, songs, paintings, sculptures, and many other works of art. It inspires us to be more, to be better, and do better than we think we are capable of. It is the glue that holds us together when we feel we are going to break. It is the warm blanket that eases our suffering during times of pain, sorrow, or loss, and it helps heal our hurts.

Although it can inspire a full range of emotions such as warmth, caring, affection, passion, adoration, compassion, empathy, goodwill, and many others love itself is not an emotion. It is an energy that flows from deep within us, from deep within our hearts. It comes from beyond this physical dimension, from beyond this world of form. It flows from the unmanifested realm of the spirit, from the Source of all things. Some call this Source God, a Higher Power, Universal Consciousness, or a multitude of other names. But love is the physical manifestation of this Source in our world. The expression "God is Love" is not entirely accurate. After all, the Source is so much more than just this physical manifestation but it certainly does point in the right direction.

As a friend of mine often says, love flows in one direction, which is outward. I believe this to be true. Love is selfless. It does not take, need, or want, it only gives. Love is neither dependent upon, nor affected by any outside source. To this end, the phrase *"unconditional love"* is a redundancy, because real love is unconditional. If it is not unconditional, then it is not love. It might be an obsession, addiction, clinging, or neediness. It might appear to be infatuation, sexual attraction, or manipulation, but these things are not love. They are selfish and contain a want, need, or desire. As I have felt and experienced it, we are the vehicle through which love is expressed in the world. Many of us are either unaware of this or dismiss the importance of it, which saddens me because it is such an honor and privilege to be the conduit through which love is shared. Love wells up and through us, flows out through our hearts into this world, and is expressed through our feelings, thoughts, and actions. Love, though formless, can assume many forms. Simple hugs; acts of consideration, care, and concern for others; gestures of selflessness, kindness, and generosity; and deeds of service to others without expectation of result or reward, without ego satisfaction, recognition, or acknowledgment, but simply because they are the right things to do are just some of the shapes love can take. Such actions give us a sense of fullness and completeness because, as this love flows through our acts, it fills our hearts. This is why giving is always more satisfying, more rewarding than taking. The age-old expression that "it is better to give than to receive" has been right all along.

Romance and sexual interaction can be and are probably most thought of as expressions of love, but they can be deceiving. The motive behind them may or may not be pure. When we are "in love," our hearts swell with this energy. It fills our bodies, leaving us flush with it coursing through us. It is what makes us feel so energetic, gives us that extra bounce in our step, and makes us feel almost invincible as if we can take on the world. The consciousness inhabiting our body is swimming in this energy. It is literally "in love". The reason this feeling can sometimes fade over time causing new love to lose its luster is most often because the person is not connected with their inner Self. The person is thus unable to summon or feel the full expanse of love that wells from within. This leaves the person relying on an outside source to fuel that love. Although love received from another feels wonderful and makes us feel special, it is fleeting and unsustainable without our own connection to love.

Love is also eternal. It transcends space and time: coming from a place where these do not exist. The proof of this is that the love we feel for others remains regardless of the distance between us and regardless of the passage of time. Even after we pass on, the love we have does not diminish or disintegrate. As mentioned earlier, love is an energy, and energy does not dissipate. It transforms. It returns to the Source from whence it and we originated. When a new body manifests, it becomes a new conduit, and the Source once again flows into this physical world as love.

So why is it that not everyone feels this way? Why is there so much anger, aggression, and violence in the world? Why do we not all love one another but often fear, hate, or envy each other? Unconscious conditioning from family and the dysfunctional society we live in, abuse and trauma we suffer both physically and psychologically, and the resulting fear and selfishness all lead us to try to "protect ourselves" by putting up walls and by closing or blocking off our hearts. Doing so starves our spirits and shrivels our hearts by disconnecting us from the Source. This disconnection forces us to live a dark, cold, lonely existence, separate from everyone else, with little or no meaningful connection with anyone. In a futile attempt to protect ourselves we are blocking and disconnecting ourselves from the one thing that can heal us—love.

The emotional neglect and lack of love and affection I experienced growing up, the trauma and conditioning I received, did just this. It forced me to recoil and separate myself from people, to develop mistrust, and to build walls to shield myself. It left me with unfathomable loneliness and sadness, riddled with fears, insecurities, and warped, often hostile perceptions of others. All the friendships or relationships I had were cold and casual or even adversarial. I kept everyone at arm's length. If someone who genuinely cared and wanted to express love grew too close, I lashed out to push them away, causing even more abuse and trauma. That loving, caring behavior was completely foreign and thus threatening to me. When I succeeded and they either pulled away to protect themselves or left entirely, it reinforced my feelings of neglect and abandonment, further perpetuating the cycle. I prevented meaningful friendships from blossoming and left many girlfriends feeling hurt, abused, and bewildered.

It was only through desperation and the pain of isolation that I cried out for help, seeking to become free from this destructive cycle. I was fortunate to meet a group of people, most of whom had experienced similar types of trauma, but had learned to overcome it. They had learned to tear down their walls. Through their shared experience, support, and encouragement of one another, they had learned to reconnect to the Source and to let love flow once again. These people wanted nothing from me but to share this precious gift. They sought only to teach me how to let go of what I had learned while trying to defend myself from all the would-be abusers and to embrace the love that had been so foreign to me for so many years. All that was asked is that once I had learned, that I too share this gift with others that have suffered. Through patience, perseverance, and practice I too have learned to tear down my walls to reconnect to the Source and to let love flow. No longer do I feel neglected and abandoned. No longer do I perceive others as threats. No longer do I feel the need to "protect" myself. The love that I have allowed to fill me and to flow through me has healed me. My only wish is that, as this love flows outward from within me, it touches your heart and awakens the love that is already within you.

The Unlearning Process

"Fill thy cup with nothing 'til it runneth over. Only then will you know peace." These words came to me this morning in a dream. I awoke with them repeating in my mind like a mantra. What I gather from them is that if I am to find and know peace, I must first unlearn and let go of all that I have known and learned. I speak, of course, of misinformation, of unhealthy and destructive behavior patterns, of distorted and inaccurate beliefs. These form the conditioning I received from the family and society I was raised in and have spent the majority of my life learning from. This had resulted in a warped perception of reality, false belief systems, and a perceived sense of threat and hostility from and towards the world. Such things had created a confused, frustrated, angered, enraged, fearful, untrusting, alienated, lonely, isolated, enigmatic person. They had created a person unable to give or receive love, a person who felt unworthy of love: a person threatened by love due to his lack of understanding of it. A person with no experience of love and so unable to express any of love's sibling sensibilities for fear of further misunderstanding, alienation, lack of reciprocity, even retaliation.

Thankfully, most days I am no longer that person. Nor do I still harbor anger or ill will toward anyone. This, however, is not something that happened spontaneously, or overnight. Breaking patterns and beliefs is rarely easy. It takes time and effort, but for me, it has been a fairly simple and straightforward process. It formed through my realization and acceptance that what I had learned is untrue, choosing to let go of those untruths, and then replacing them with the truth. It doesn't always happen in that order though. Sometimes the light of truth is required to reveal the untruth. Whichever way the process unfolds, the result is the same: freedom.

So, let me now share with you the greatest untruths that I had learned and the subsequent unlearning of them.

1. I am different and there is something wrong with me.

> This goes way back to the very beginning. I was born slightly crippled with what they called a "club foot." My right foot was turned in at almost a 90-degree angle. The only solution at the time was to gradually bend the leg back into place and set it properly. As an infant, I was fortunate that the bones were still soft enough to accomplish this over a 6-month span. It required wearing a series of three casts. I wore a leg brace for two years afterward, just to ensure the leg stayed in proper alignment. The leg healed but emerged from the process weaker and more delicate than my left leg. Since then I have broken that very same ankle on four separate occasions, resulting in two major reconstructive surgeries. To experience such trauma as

a newborn and with no ability to express one's feelings, there was nowhere else for the pain to go but inward. I suffered horrible nightmares and would thrash about so violently in my sleep that I would throw myself out of bed. My parents had to install bars on the sides of my bed, much like those on a hospital bed, to keep me from falling out. Perhaps they thought I was too young to understand. Perhaps I was, but I recall having received nothing else from them in the way of help, explanation, console, or comfort. So, in my earliest, most formative years, when it is said that we learn more than we do during the remainder of our lives, I learned this deep-seated untruth. I always felt damaged, as if I would never be as good as anyone else, no matter how hard I tried. I also learned that I would always be different, that I would never quite fit in. With friends and peers, I always felt apart, alienated. None of them had experienced the trauma I had, so they could never understand me.

This untruth stayed with me through childhood, adolescence, and adulthood. It remained with me until I learned, through spiritual searching and practice, who I truly am, and that physical differences or even handicaps are only skin deep. I learned that below the surface, in essence, we are all the same. We are all connected, all coming from the same source. So how could I possibly be different from anyone else? In this physical manifestation, I am human as are we all. I am perfectly imperfect, and there is nothing wrong with that. This is the truth that has replaced the untruth.

2. I cannot trust anyone, and I am on my own.

Having already felt the alienation from the first untruth, this one was not far behind. When I was about six, my oldest sister found her adoption papers, which my parents had kept hidden from her. It turned out that she was only my half-sister, that we had different fathers, and that when my father had married my mother he had adopted her as his own. There is nothing wrong with this; it happens all the time. I even consider it a loving gesture on my father's part. The harm in it is that they kept it hidden, never telling her or any of us about it. When my sister found the papers, she undoubtedly and justifiably snapped, yelling and cursing them for their deception, creating a big scene. In an attempt to put a Band-Aid on the bullet wound this situation had become, my parents dragged all of us into family therapy to try to address and resolve the issue. Because I was so young, I don't recall much other than all of my sisters crying and being very upset while I had the disturbing feeling that my parents had done something very wrong. If anyone had asked me then how I felt about it, I doubt I would have had the ability to express my feelings. In retrospect, what I took away from that experience was that my parents were dishonest and deceitful and could not be trusted. If my parents—the two people who brought me into this world, who I've looked to for love, affection, instruction, and guidance, who were tasked with raising, nurturing, and caring for me—were untrustworthy, then how could I ever trust anyone else? I simply could not. I needed to fend for myself. Thus the second untruth was born.

This untruth had been the source of much of the isolation I had felt as well as the foundation for the emotional walls I had constructed to protect myself. Also, the false belief that I am self-sufficient, that I need no one, and that anything that needs to be done can and must be done by me alone, grew from this untruth. Shortly after this experience occurred, I stole for the first time. I grabbed twenty dollars from my mother's purse, went running out the door and down the block toward the candy store, believing that if I wanted something I would have to get it myself. I got grabbed up by one of my neighbors and returned to my mother, who spanked and scolded me. I did not, however, learn that what I did was wrong. Nor did I feel any remorse. I only felt that I needed to get better at it if I were to succeed in supporting myself. This untruth had also infected most of my friendships and relationships, and was often the cause of their demise, for I had become incapable of letting anyone in. It had also been the cause of much of my suffering as I could no longer ask for help when it was needed.

I did not begin to unlearn this untruth until I began to let my walls down and let people in. With faith, trust, and courage I started to become a little vulnerable and let people love me, care for me, and support me. I realized that I was not alone and that people could indeed be trusted. This realization replaced the untruth. In accepting my humanity with all its flaws, I have allowed others the space to be human as well. I realized that they will sometimes make mistakes or let me down, but that they rarely do so with malice or mal-intent. I also realized that I can forgive others as I have learned to forgive myself. I have since been able to develop close, meaningful, and loving relationships with people I can trust and rely on. I hold these near and dear to my heart.

3. Nothing I do will ever be good enough.

I can attribute this one mostly to the relationship with my mother. She was an extremely negative and critical woman. I am aware of the upbringing she had and the circumstances of her life that molded and shaped her so I hold no grudge. Like most of us, myself included, she was a product of the conditioning she had received. Unfortunately, though, my sense of forbearance does not erase the damage her negativity caused. No matter how hard I tried, my efforts never seemed to be enough for her. If I got a 90 on a test, why didn't I get a 100? Even on the occasion when I did everything right, instead of "Congratulations" or "Good job," I got "Well it's about time. This is what you should've been doing in the first place." Maybe, in her mind, she was encouraging me to try harder, to strive to do better and be better, but all she succeeded in doing was destroying my self-esteem and instilling in me an irrational need to be perfect. Because

I am human and therefore fallible, becoming perfect was unattainable. The effort, however, left me constantly feeling like a failure and like someone who does not and never will measure up.

This "perfectionism" perpetuated the untruth that my mother had instilled in me. No matter what accomplishments I gained, no matter which goals I achieved, it was never enough. I could never fully appreciate or enjoy my successes or, God forbid, give myself a pat on the back for a job well done. Nor could I accept compliments or congratulations from anyone else. Whenever I inevitably failed or fell short of my unrealistic goals, it just tore away at my already damaged self-esteem and self-worth. It had also made me similar to her: negative, critical of, and unfairly judgmental toward others.

It has taken many years to undo the damage caused by this untruth, but through an understanding of humility and the practice of selfless service, I have been able to replace it. I no longer suffer the need to be perfect, nor do I expect perfection in others.

I know I will never be perfect. I also know I do not have to be. This realization has granted me the ability to accept my humanity. It has also taught me to accept the humanity in others: to allow them the grace to make mistakes, to refrain from judging them. So long as I try, so long as I give my best effort, I know that I have done all I can and that it is enough. Today I can appreciate my accomplishments. I can accept the praise and admiration of others. I can also offer that praise and admiration to others for their accomplishments. I no longer beat myself up when I fall short. I take those moments as the gifts that they are: opportunities to grow and to learn. The effort has become more important than the outcome, more important than results.

Serving selflessly, giving of myself to help others, and expecting nothing in return has facilitated the healing of my damaged self-esteem. Such acts support me in feeling worthwhile because they are expressions of love, compassion, and goodwill. Permitting such positive energy to flow through me has helped wash away negativity and critical thinking. This has filled me with love, allowing me to be gentle with myself and others. It has allowed me to appreciate myself as the kind, caring, and considerate person I have become.

4. I am undeserving or unworthy of love.

Imagine a sensitive, emotional boy born into a cold, dry, unexpressive family. Right from the beginning, the boy feels he is different—that there's something wrong with him. After all, his self-esteem is damaged due to a negative, critical mother who is never satisfied and who never offers praise or admiration. Next, pile onto the boy feelings of isolation and separation resulting from the walls of mistrust he has built around his sensitivity. What you have is the formula for yet another untruth. You wind up with a boy who has never felt loved, a boy who has come to the untruthful conclusion that he is somehow unworthy or undeserving of that love.

This is how and where I wound up as a result of the emotional neglect and psychological damage that occurred during my childhood. Scared, alone, and misunderstood, I felt as if the people who were supposed to love me were untrustworthy. I felt they were the ones causing me harm. I was forced to harden myself, to protect myself. I created a defensive space of emotional distance between myself and them. I began to bury my feelings. Feelings, after all, seemed a weakness, a source of vulnerability, so I hid them away. Although doing so made me feel safer, it reinforced my feelings of isolation. Unbeknownst to me, for years to come, this hardening process was the very thing that prevented me from feeling loved.

I closed my heart to protect myself. Doing so, though, cut me off from love: both the giving and receiving of it. Having been raised in an unloving environment, I did not understand what love was or where it came from. By closing my heart, I prevented the love that emanates from deep within us, from the Source, to flow up into me and out through me as it is meant to. The absence of that love, that vibrant, healing energy, left me empty and cold. So much so that when anyone tried to share their love with me, it felt alien and threatening. So I unconsciously pushed them away, leaving me to feel rejected and alone again, not realizing that I was the one causing it, inadvertently and cyclically reinforcing this untruth.

Eventually, I reached a tipping point. The damage caused by this destructive cycle began to outweigh its perceived protective benefits. The need for connection surpassed the need to isolate and prevent anyone from getting close. Slowly, gradually, and with the help of some loving, caring, genuine people, I began to chip away at the protective shell I had placed around my heart. In doing so, I learned that the love I so desperately needed had been inside me all along. It had simply been blocked by my defenses. As this love began to flow up through me and out, filling me in the process, my broken spirit began to heal. The walls I had constructed to protect myself began to crumble. They were no longer needed, allowing me to love myself and others and let others love me. I no longer feel unworthy or undeserving of love. Nor should anyone. It is through loving one another that we help each other heal, and heal ourselves as well.

5. Love is a weapon, and people will only hurt you.

This is another untruth I had learned through an accumulation of painful experiences and negative reinforcement. Having suffered through a childhood of emotional neglect and constant negativity, I already believed that people were dangerous and that they would hurt me if given the opportunity. It was a hostile, stressful, fearful way to grow up. I was constantly guarded and on edge, always poised and ready to defend against attack. My first romantic relationship contributed to this perceived need to protect myself. It was the first time I experienced how love can be used as a weapon to hurt me.

Her name was Teresa. She was half African American, half Puerto Rican, already fully developed and beautiful at fourteen years of age. I too was fourteen. For the first time, I experienced feelings of affection and desire. After all that I had been through, was it possible that this girl, this beautiful young woman, actually wanted me, wanted to care for me, and could maybe even love me? We enjoyed two weeks of blissful puppy love, which is nearly a lifetime at fourteen. I had let my guard down and allowed her to love me as I loved her. It was exhilarating and exciting, and I started to have hope that everything might be okay after all. Then one night, a bunch of us were hanging out behind the Board of Education building in my neighborhood, as we often did. I was talking to a girl whose name I cannot even remember. I will admit she was cute and that I was attracted to her, but we were just talking, hanging out like everyone else was. Along came Teresa, who saw me talking to this other girl. She flipped out, screaming at me, accusing me of cheating on her. I tried to talk to her and calm her down and reassure her that nothing was going on, but she would not be swayed. She broke up with me on the spot and stormed away. Looking back, I can see clearly that Teresa carried some pain of her own: mistrust, insecurity, and suspicion from either past relationships or family. At the time, however, I was naïve about all that. I was devastated as if she had just ripped my heart out of my chest. It was a pain and a feeling of rejection I could not bear. I had protected myself for so long, and the one time I let my guard down and let someone into my heart, that special someone had stomped all over it and had thrown it away. It was the first time I wanted to die. I was ill-equipped to deal with such intense feelings, thus the breakup was the cause of my only suicide attempt. Thankfully, it was a feeble one. I tried to cut my wrist with a little, dull pocketknife. I stopped, though, because it hurt and I realized that what I was attempting was stupid. Having discovered how dangerous love was, how it could be used to hurt and destroy me, I vowed to myself that no one would ever hurt me like that again.

I kept every subsequent relationship or love interest at arm's length. I became the manipulator, using love to get what I wanted. I would keep girlfriends close enough for them to stay interested, but far enough away that they could never hurt me. Anyone who genuinely cared or loved me received the worst of it, suffering emotional whiplash from the barrage of mixed messages I sent out. I destroyed many relationships and hurt so many beautiful, gentle, loving people. Each time I felt worse and worse about myself for inflicting the kind of pain I had experienced. But I also felt trapped by the fear of getting hurt again. I must admit that this type of behavior went on well into adulthood, well into the midst of my spiritual journey. The behavior patterns that had developed as a result of this untruth were so deeply ingrained that they would activate almost automatically, making them extremely difficult to stop or prevent.

Once again, love, not the manipulating weapon that I thought it was, but the beautiful, healing energy that it is, became the solution to unlearning this poisonous, destructive untruth. From those who wanted nothing from me but to see me heal, I learned that often when people hurt each other, it is a result of conditioning, of learned behavior. Certainly, it was in my case. I was hurt initially by others and learned to hurt others as a response or defense, causing the same type of pain I had originally experienced. Now I break away from this cycle of hurt by seeing people for who they are, not for the way they behave. I realize today that we all have baggage, just like I did, just like Teresa did. I know now that, despite the way many of us have been conditioned, we are innately all kind, gentle souls. We search for connection and look to be loved. I know that if I want to be loved, I must love. I must offer people the same grace that I have been given. I must give them the space to heal and grow. The love I can express now is neither conditional nor a tool for manipulation. It is pure—without strings or restrictions.

6. Escape is the only solution and solace.

Having never been taught how to deal with my emotions nor with the baggage I had carried since early childhood, I sought my only solution—escape. As a child, I escaped through fantasy, stories, cartoons, comics, as well as food and drink. Cookies, cakes, and candies offered an exhilarating sugar rush. When nobody was looking, I even went so far as to sneak spoonfuls of sugar right from the sugar bowl. During parties and family gatherings, I would go from table to table sneaking sips of beer and wine until I was tipsy. I would act silly and roll around on the floor, and everyone laughed and thought it was the cutest thing. But I was just enjoying the sweet taste of freedom from the way I felt. By my teenage years, I had been introduced to illicit substances. The very first time I got high I felt as if I had found what had always been missing from my life. For the first time, the fear, the doubt, the insecurity, the negativity, the mistrust were all gone. Oblivion became my best friend as I decided to just stay high all the time.

Substance abuse, although effective at numbing me and giving me a sense of relief, came with its own set of problems. Dependency, the need for more and more, the eternal search for ways and means to get more, lying, cheating, stealing, and manipulation were all results of my substance abuse. These destructive behaviors created guilt, remorse, and shame, which also needed to be numbed, thus perpetuating the downward spiral of addiction. Eventually, the pain of the consequences grew greater than the pain I felt inside and I cried out for help.

Once clean, I no longer suffered the pain and consequences of using. The old, familiar pain of emotions and dealing with myself and my baggage had returned, though. Fortunately, I had been introduced to a fellowship of people who had suffered as I had, who felt the way I did, and who had found a real solution, not a temporary respite. As I embarked on the road to recovery, I began to learn healthy and constructive ways to deal with myself and the world around me. Recovery, though, is a process that takes time, so the desire to escape lingered. The ways of escaping became more subtle, more insidious. I would find escape once again in food, in sex, in adrenaline-inducing activities, and in mind games such as imaginary conversations and relationships I would play out in my head, rather than dealing with people in reality. Escape, however, no longer worked the way it used to. It did not compliment this new life I was living. It only hindered it. I learned through sometimes difficult lessons that the only way to be free of pain is to simply go through it. I learned that dealing with my feelings, with life, and with the world around me is easier and way more rewarding than running away. The only time I now have difficulty is when I get duped by my mind into thinking that the old ways are better. When this happens, the old thought and behavior patterns pop up. Fortunately, as time goes on and my recovery progresses, this happens less and less. Reality has become exciting and exhilarating, full of opportunities to love and to share with those in my life whose presence I cherish. This final untruth has been replaced.

Today I live a life of honesty, of truth, of love, of care, of trust in myself and others: a life of meaning, purpose, and fulfillment. I live a life I no longer wish to escape from but am present in and enjoy fully. I am forever grateful for the unlearning process and shall continue practicing these truths through the remainder of my days.

The Breadth of Breath

We breathe in, we breathe out, and our breath feeds us the oxygen our bodies need to survive, to thrive, and to grow, yet breathing goes far beyond this biological function.

We breathe in, we breathe out, and our breath is automatic, governed by an intelligence far greater than our own. Breathing is so simple that it is easily overlooked, and yet it is as important as the heartbeat for giving and sustaining life.

We breathe in, we breathe out, and our breath offers us a precious pause between thought and action, between emotion and action: a moment that can spare us and others the pain of rash reaction.

We breathe in, we breathe out, and our breath offers us a moment of relief from the heaviness of the world, a temporary respite during times of trouble, difficulty, pain, or sorrow. This moment allows us a chance to recompose ourselves, and once again to rise to the challenge.

We breathe in, we breathe out, and our breath anchors us to the moment, bringing our awareness to the here and now. If we give attention to the breath and follow it, it frees us from the chains of the mind and its playgrounds of past and future.

We breathe in, we breathe out, and our breath attunes us to our inner energy flowing through our body. We gain a sense of vibrancy and liveliness.

We breathe in, we breathe out, and our breath serves as a gateway to the universe beyond the one we see, smell, taste, touch, and hear, to the one we feel deep within, to the place of Knowing.

We breathe in, we breathe out, and our breath tethers us to our body so that our spirit may journey through sleep, dream, and meditation to the unmanifested realm, never fearing that it might get lost and not find its way back home.

We breathe in, we breathe out ... we breathe in, we breathe out ... we breathe in, we breathe out ... and we are free.

The Weight of Waiting

We wait for the kettle or pot to boil, or for the toaster, the microwave, or the oven to finish. We wait for our breakfast, our lunch, our dinner to be ready, whether prepared by us or by another. Or we wait in the restaurant for the waiter to take our order, to bring us our food, to bring us the check. We sit at the red light, waiting for it to change, or behind someone waiting for them to make a left, or in traffic waiting for it to clear. We wait while standing in line at the bank, the supermarket, the post office, or the dreaded DMV, the Dominion of the Moment Vultures who steal away precious moments of our lives.

We cannot wait for the workday to be over, for Friday, or the weekend. We cannot wait for a day off or tonight, to hang out with our friends or to kick off our shoes, put our feet up and relax at home. We cannot wait for the next episode of our favorite show, or for that new movie to come out, or for our favorite holiday to arrive, or to take that vacation, or to find that new job, or that new girlfriend, boyfriend, husband, or wife. We cannot wait to buy that new car or bike, or those new clothes, or that new piece of furniture, or the latest electronic gadget. We cannot wait for our plans to come to fruition or to be successful. All of these things that we "can't wait for," we, of course, wait for because they all take place in the future, and we must wait for them to arrive. We wait and wait and wait.

How many times have we waited for something to happen or arrive, which never does? Or how many times has that event or moment arrived, only for it to not prove as exciting or satisfying as we had anticipated? Or there are those rare occasions that what we have long thought about or planned or dreamed does arrive or occur, and it is fulfilling and satisfying or even beyond what we had anticipated. How long do we spend enjoying the spoils of that victory, that achievement, that materialization of our dreams and desires before our minds are looking ahead to the next thing to wait for, robbing us of that moment? If we stop and think about it, how much of our lives do we waste waiting? How many moments have accumulated and added up to hours, days, weeks, months, or maybe even years? Huge chunks of our lives, never to be regained or lived again, have gone to waiting. Well, I am here to tell you, my friends, that the wait is over if you so choose.

I no longer bear the weight of waiting. I shrug it off and refuse it. I no longer wait for the kettle to boil. I prepare the tea. I wash the dirty dishes in the sink, even if they are but a few. I put away the clean dishes from the dish rack into the cupboard. Or I otherwise occupy that time, not for it to simply pass but to make more efficient use of it, to live it. I do not wait for the red light to change or the traffic to subside. I enjoy the song on the radio, or I breathe and bring my attention to the breath so I can center myself and enjoy the present moment. Then I observe my surroundings. I take in the beauty of the world around me: the beauty that so often had gone undetected. I no longer wait for that special event to arrive, for that vacation day, or the new job, car, girl, or house. I do not wait for success to find me or for my dreams to be realized. I embrace what I have, what exists in the here and now. I find gratitude and appreciation for it. Does this mean that I no longer cherish dreams or aspirations? I do, but to reach them I make plans and envision goals as well as the steps to achieve them. No longer are the goals my primary concern, though. They are secondary. What's primary is the step I take right here, right now. The step that leads toward that goal.

I am speaking of living in the moment, in the here and now. Not in some future that has not manifested, that exists only in the mind. I live in reality, embracing each moment as it arrives, not before. Just because some future event or circumstance holds the allure of excitement and happiness does not mean that those things cannot be found here and now. By being present, I find real joy, beauty, and excitement in every moment, not in some fantasy, some perceived future moment yet to arrive. Even writing these letters and syllables I do here and now: the words unfolding, from this moment to the next. I do not write looking to the book's completion or its publishing in some nearby or distant future, to some "when" that is only anticipated. I write now, in this very moment. I write to you, my friend, who reads these words at this moment. I say to you, this is the moment, your moment. Embrace it now. Live it now. Experience the exhilaration of watching the universe and life itself unfold before your eyes. Wait no more.

The Tree of Life

"We are, in essence, the same being, all branches of the Tree of Life." Yes, I did just quote myself from a previous chapter. While it may seem a bit narcissistic to do so, that line is the inspiration for this chapter. So what better place to begin?

The Tree of Life is, of course, not an actual, physical tree but an ethereal one. It is a metaphor, a representation, and a fairly accurate one at that. It is the eternal life force that permeates all of existence: giving life to everything in it. Sprouted from its roots, from the Source, the Tree grows. The roots give life to life, enabling the Tree to be. They nurture the tree, enabling it to flourish. From here the Tree of Life branches out in an infinite number of directions. Each branch is a life unto itself, not separate from the tree but One with it. It is an extension of the Tree: a part of the whole. Each branch, in turn, sprouts leaves, also not separate from the branch, nor the Tree, but an extension of them: a temporary manifestation.

Now imagine if we were to give those leaves a mind enabling them to be self-aware, enabling them to think, to reason, to create incredible beauty, to invent impressive and useful technology, to better the quality of their lives and their experience of living it. Marveling at their magnificence of creativity and ingenuity, their self-awareness can easily become self-absorption, self-obsession, ego, and arrogance. The leaves could easily forget that they are but an extension of the branch. They can begin to feel separate from it, even forgetting that the branch exists in the first place. When this perceived separation occurs, the trouble begins. Differentiation begins to take hold: "Those leaves are different from me. They're a different color, this one's bigger than me, that one's smaller than me, they're a different shape than me." This all furthers the feeling of separation, bringing a sense of isolation, of aloneness. What is worse is that the self-awareness also brings with it the realization that the leaves' existence is a temporary one, subject to the cycle of birth and death. Being faced with their mortality brings them a tremendous fear of impending doom, anxiety, and worry.

While this may be an imagined scenario regarding the leaves, this is what has happened to us for generations upon generations and continues to happen today in our society. We are branches who have mistaken ourselves for leaves. We have forgotten our roots, and are aware only of our physical selves. We live in our bodies, taking them to be who we are. Either we have completely forgotten the eternal life force flowing within or we have grown so distant from it, so duped by the misperception created by the ego, that we cannot find our way back home to it. We live our lives seemingly separate from everyone and everything else and are riddled with anxiety, insecurity, and worry because our fear of death permeates every thought and action.

Let me ask you this, though: When the leaves eventually wither and die and fall to the ground, does the branch look down upon them and think, "My leaves are dead and gone. Life is over, and I am no more"? Of course, it doesn't. The branch knows that its leaves are but a temporary manifestation. It knows that it is a part of the Tree and that life is eternal. It knows that although it may lie dormant for a time through the winter, eventually spring will come and it will once again sprout leaves. When we "die," our physical form remains, yet people still say that "we're gone." If that is so, then who are we? It is clear that we are not the body, because it is still there. We are that eternal life force that was inhabiting the body. The only place we have gone from is that physical manifestation. We are still the branch that is connected to the Tree of Life. We've simply shed our leaves, our physical form.

To be free from the illusion that our ego has created—that we are no more than just our bodies—and all the fear, doubt, worry, and isolation that accompanies that illusion, we need only realize that we are the branch, the life force that is a part of the eternal Tree. Our physical form is only a temporary extension of that life force. We are connected to every other branch, every other being, not separate, not alone. The difference in our foliage is insignificant. We are all One: all part of the same Tree of Life.

Sadhana

Sadhana, for those who do not know, is the means, instrument, or practice for spiritual growth. As I have mentioned previously, I do not follow any specific religion or spiritual discipline. However, this particular word—Sadhana—and what it represents resonates with me. It does not mean "meditation" specifically, although meditation can be Sadhana. It refers to whatever practice helps facilitate or move you along in your journey towards your goal.

So, with that in mind...

When I wake in the morning and I put a smile on because I am graced with another day ... that is my Sadhana.

When I get up and make the bed ... that is my Sadhana.

When I recite my morning prayers and sit for meditation ... that is my Sadhana.

When I put the kettle on and prepare my morning tea ... that is my Sadhana.

When I drink the tea ... that is my Sadhana.

When I sit and read ... that is my Sadhana.

When I sit at the computer, become absorbed in social media, and before I know it an hour has slipped away and now I have to rush ... that is my Sadhana. Thankfully, this does not happen all the time because it is a difficult Sadhana when it does.

When I prepare breakfast and a lunch to take to work ... that is my Sadhana.

When I eat breakfast ... that is my Sadhana.

When I do the dishes ... that is my Sadhana.

When I go to the bathroom ... that is my Sadhana.

When I take a shower ... that is my Sadhana.

When I get dressed and ready to go to work ... that is my Sadhana.

When I drive to work ... that is my Sadhana.

When I am driving and someone cuts in front of me or drives slowly or does something that I might find disagreeable ... that is my Sadhana.

When I chop vegetables or make the sauce at work ... that is my Sadhana.

When I go make a delivery ... that is my Sadhana.

When I eat my lunch ... that is my Sadhana.

When I have conversations with my coworkers or my boss or customers or anyone I meet in my travels ... that is my Sadhana.

When I leave work to drive home ... that is my Sadhana.

When I get home, change out of my work clothes, prepare and drink another cup of tea ... these are all my Sadhana.

When I prepare dinner ... that is my Sadhana.

When I eat dinner ... that is my Sadhana.

When I go to a meeting ... that is my Sadhana.

When I choose to help others through selfless service ... that is my Sadhana.

When I choose to be selfish and help no one ... that is my Sadhana.

When I go out with friends and, eat, talk, and laugh with them ... that is my Sadhana.

When I drive home ... that is my Sadhana.

When I get home, prepare for bed, and express gratitude for another day, another opportunity to live life ... that is my Sadhana.

Throughout my day, when I remember my breath and give attention to it ... that is my Sadhana.

When I give attention to my true self, the inner self, and feel the life energy flowing through my body ... that is my Sadhana.

When I forget my breath, forget myself, and get caught up in my thoughts or my ego or otherwise get distracted ... that is my Sadhana. Yet another difficult, sometimes painful one but my Sadhana nonetheless.

When I have to get up in the middle of the night out of a sound sleep to pee because, as I grow older, this seems to be a thing that happens ... that is my Sadhana.

Now, at this point, you may be asking yourself or you may be ready to ask me, "How can all of those things be your Sadhana?" Well, hopefully asking that question, at the moment of asking, that becomes your Sadhana. But I will answer with this ...

Remaining anchored in the present moment and having present moment awareness is my Sadhana, so anything that finds its way into the present moment then becomes my Sadhana for that moment. So, as I have described, whenever any of these activities arise in the present moment, they then become my Sadhana. Everything that occurs throughout the day can be my Sadhana if I pay attention. Even writing this book, in this very moment of the writing … that is my Sadhana. Some days I do quite well with my Sadhana, and my day is filled with love, compassion, joy, excitement, and exhilaration. Some days, as mentioned above, I become distracted and I cause pain and suffering for myself and those around me. On those days, though, that suffering is my Sadhana, and some of the most valuable lessons I have ever learned have come from my suffering.

As I have learned, the present moment is the only moment that truly exists, so it is of utmost importance that I learn to live in it and practice paying attention to it. So that is my Sadhana because I desire to live freely. Free from my mind and its illusions. Its illusions of past and future, its illusions of false selves and ego, its illusions of separation and differentiation, its illusions of impermanence and death. I seek to be free of it all. I seek to know the truth, to know who I am and, in turn, know everyone else—because we are all One—so that I can be free of me so that I can just simply be. This is my goal. To move towards it I must practice presence in the here and now. So … that is my Sadhana.

Family Healing

I attended a family dinner last night to celebrate my dad's birthday. It was a relatively small gathering: just me, my dad, his wife, my aunt, and my uncle. This was great for me because large gatherings still tend to wear me out or overwhelm me. The barrage of surface conversations coupled with more than enough food to bury any uncomfortable feelings that might materialize often leaves me bloated, drained, and feeling like an outsider. Small talk has never been my strong suit. I am frequently left wondering how I'm even part of the family when I feel so distant and so isolated from them. For many years I wouldn't even attend such gatherings, finding one excuse or another for my absence. I would say that I had to work, had a prior engagement, or was not feeling up to it. I knew full and well that these excuses were not true or were simply offered as a matter of convenience. When I did attend, mostly out of a feeling of obligation, I would usually seek out another guest who also seemed like an outsider. This would usually be my brother-in-law, and we got along very well. We would sit off to the side and either observe or engage in a separate conversation so that we would not feel so alone.

This was a much smaller, more manageable, and intimate gathering though. Much to my surprise and delight, it was not filled with a multitude of mundane conversations. I did not have to just suffer through it, occasionally interjecting a witty, comedic remark giving the appearance that I was part of the conversation rather an outsider awkwardly looking in. It was filled with enlightening and engaging conversations about an assortment of spiritual practices and disciplines, book recommendations, meditation, and soul searching. It addressed emotional and psychological trauma and spiritual healing. It was thrilling to partake in conversations of substance, and I began to realize that there are parts of my family that are evolving and growing spiritually. I knew my uncle had. He had left the corporate world after over twenty years and had become a yoga instructor: more for spiritual growth and healing rather than for the simple physical exercise. I admired him for that. He had also previously recommended spiritual literature to me and had taught me some healing exercises. So he had already been an inspiration and had helped me along my path. For my dad's birthday, I gave him a copy of Eckhart Tolle's *The Power of Now*, thinking it might help propel him into awakening, into spiritual life. Much to my surprise, he told me that, although he had not read that book, he had watched some of his videos online and was familiar with him. My aunt also chimed in that she had read his material for years and thoroughly enjoyed his teachings. Both my aunt and uncle went on to tell me about and recommend many other books and authors who I could look into. I was humbled and happy to see members of my family in this new light. It has helped me to acknowledge and strip away yet another ego-created false identity of being the only member of my family who has grown and evolved. I am happy to be free of that false identity and my ego, to look at myself once again and see a deeper truth.

It was also a joy to watch as the three siblings spoke of experiences from their past, and of their life together. I realized that they are indeed a family, not just a group of strangers who happened to have been lumped together by biology. Because of my distorted perception, this is how I had always perceived my family. But they had grown up together, shared experiences, shared time, shared love, and participated in each other's lives. They made the effort to maintain their relationships all through the years, regardless of distance or whatever direction their lives had taken. Seeing this and seeing them in this new light has again made me look at myself, reflect on my life, and acknowledge that most of the isolation I have felt was of my own making. I had already learned this to some extent, but experiencing them in this way has helped solidify that lesson. I am not looking to minimize, discount, or dismiss the trauma I experienced growing up, but the defenses and walls I had developed in an attempt to protect myself are the very things that kept me feeling alone, isolated, and apart from my family. These people have grown, evolved, and healed as I have. The only thing that has prevented me from being a part of that and experiencing it with them is me. Like many of the unhealthy, destructive habits and behaviors I developed growing up, the illusion that I needed to protect myself and distance myself from them no longer has a place in my life. To know that there are at least a few members of my family with who I can connect on an emotional and spiritual level is a blessing. Hopefully, this knowledge will help me to drop any other false perceptions that may still linger. I hope that I now have the clarity to see my family as they are today, not as I have perceived them based on my childhood trauma. I also hope that this experience can help foster more intimate relationships with other family members as well.

As an addendum but still appropriate to the context of this chapter, I want to add that a few weeks later was my thirtieth recovery celebration. My youngest sister, the one I have always been closest to, had baked me a cake for the celebration. While I was at her house picking it up, on a whim, I decided to invite her to the celebration. After coming off the experience I had recently with other family members, I thought I would include her in a part of my life that none of my family has been a part of for many years. The last time she attended one of my anniversaries had been twenty-four years prior. So she agreed and attended the celebration which was beautiful, full of love, and full of the people I hold nearest and dearest to my heart. I didn't have a chance to speak with her afterward, so I took the opportunity to have that conversation with her the following Monday while I was at her house doing my laundry. I asked her how she liked it and what her thoughts were. She told me she enjoyed it and that it was nice to meet in person many of my friends she had known only through social media posts. Then I told her that my intention for inviting her was for her to see the kind of person I had become, to see the change that had taken place over the years. A change that I felt would be much more impactful to experience first-hand than if I were to try to explain it to her. She replied, much to my surprise, "I know the kind of person you've become." I went on to say that

I knew communication was not a strong suit in our family and that I thought it would be better for her to see it for herself. My sister's reply struck me, as did the comments people had shared at the anniversary about how giving and loving I am towards others, and about how selflessly I have served. It reminded me that people do not see me the way I think they do, and they do not see me the way I see myself. I realized that the image I had of myself was skewed. It was a false image. I now know that the change which has taken place in my life does not need to be explained. It shows in the way I live.

She went on to share with me her experience with cancer. She was able to identify with me and my addiction through her experience with her illness. She told me about the fear, the anxiety, and the suffering it had caused in her life, as well as the eventual realization that we are all on borrowed time. She explained how this realization had enabled her to be grateful for every day that she wakes up. I was floored by her ability to articulate feelings and to express gratitude as well as her ability to relate to me on a deep level. Once again, my distorted perceptions were stripped away. I was able to see her in a new light. I am profoundly grateful for this, as it has removed yet another barrier between me and my family: one that I had again created through my misperception. It has opened the door for better communication between us and a more intimate relationship with her moving forward.

I have to express gratitude that I keep having healing experiences with my family to add as addendums to this chapter. That being said, I had a conversation with my mother the other night. Admittedly, it was a one-sided conversation because my mother has been dead since 1996. Through reading and learning though, I have come to understand that she is still alive in me. Through shared blood, shared DNA, and shared consciousness, my mother is always a part of me as I am a part of her.

With an image of her in my mind, through meditation, I brought her into the present moment with me and spoke to her. I told her I understood that the suffering she had caused me was a result of the suffering she had experienced in her own life, through the conditioning that was passed on to her by her family. I told her I understood that she had no choice, that she was never taught how to embrace her suffering and transform it so that it wouldn't be passed on and inflicted on others. I forgave her for it and asked for forgiveness for the suffering I had caused her in my ignorance and unskillfulness. I also acknowledged that it was not just suffering I received from her, but good qualities as well. My tenacity, my determination, my high pain tolerance were all good traits I had received from her. Those traits had enabled me to persevere, to struggle, to fight, and to push through all of the baggage I had accumulated to eventually find my true self. I then told her that I found what our family had been lacking for generations: a way out, a way to break the cycle, a way to not pass on my suffering but to embrace it and transform it into compassion, understanding, and kindness. I told her that I would not only do this for me and future generations, but also her, her parents, and everyone else along the line who had similarly suffered so that we could all be free. Then I told her I loved her. Words that had rarely, if ever been uttered from my lips to her. Until recently I was incapable of doing so or at least I believed I was. I now know that love—the love I feel for her, the love I feel for all of us who have suffered, the love that is constantly burning in my heart and flowing outward—is the energy that will heal us all.

Fan and Sword

As previously mentioned, I have taken bits and pieces from various teachers and disciplines along my journey. One such piece I picked up from the book *The Miracle of Mindfulness*, by Thich Nhat Hanh. Of the many things I gained from reading it, the seemingly small and simple but incredibly powerful and effective "Buddha's half-smile" has become an integral part of my spiritual practice. It has helped me more than I could have anticipated or imagined. The iconic image of Buddha sitting while donning the half-smile has been depicted, displayed, and described more times than I can imagine. In the interest of preventing redundancy, I have been hesitant to write about it. However, as with all of the writing in this book, if the inspiration to write about something strikes me, I listen and follow through.

For anyone not yet familiar with the half-smile, please know it is not so much an outward smile reflecting happiness, joy, fun, or laughter. It is a more inward smile that is barely noticeable. A smile more of feeling than of visual perception. It is a smile of acceptance of what is. A smile of understanding and compassion.

A smile of contentment and peace. In my spiritual practice, I have come to call it the Fan and Sword.

Ever since I experienced my awakening, I have had the feeling of a burning fire in my chest. I have previously explained this sensation as love, the physical manifestation of the Source. It is a powerful and healing energy that flows through me as it does all of us. Many remain unaware of this Self-love though. As a result of some sort of trauma or painful experience, they have shut themselves off from it as I had done for many years. This fire varies in intensity, based on my emotional and spiritual condition at any given moment. It can be felt as powerfully as roaring flames or as mildly as smoldering embers. When I remember to half-smile, the half-smile becomes the fan. It fans that flame in my heart. I instantly feel a flood of energy pouring into my chest as the smoldering embers reignite, growing into a flame that begins to roar with increasing intensity.

At times when I feel stressed, when I've gotten caught up in events, overwhelmed by emotion, or when mentally I've been pulled out of the moment into the past or future and have become absorbed in worry or regret, the half-smile then becomes the sword. When I remember to don the half-smile during those times, it slices through the seriousness of whatever situation I am in, whatever emotions I am feeling, and whatever thoughts are running through my mind. In an instant, or within a few conscious breaths, the half-smile reminds me that the seriousness is my creation, usually as a result of some judgment I have made or some dissatisfaction I am experiencing. I am not saying that I avoid my feelings or that I minimize or dismiss things. The half-smile simply reminds me of the lightheartedness and playfulness of the game of life. It radiates a knowingness that nothing needs to be taken so seriously that it causes unneeded suffering.

The half-smile has even gone beyond these two symbols, these two spiritual tools. The half-smile has become so entwined with and connected to the present moment that it has become an indicator or red flag. Whenever I notice I have lost the half-smile, almost without fail I've lost touch with the present moment and have either been distracted by some outside source or pulled into my mind and caught up in thought. Conversely, if I find myself distracted by thoughts, feelings, or some outside circumstance, I can surely bet that the half-smile has disappeared from my face.

The Miracle of Mindfulness speaks of donning the half-smile when first waking, during free moments, while listening to music, while doing chores, whenever irritated (this one is huge), while walking, while sitting, while focusing on the breath, while meditating, and so on and so on. Basically, during any activity or lack thereof, whenever I attempt to be mindful of the present moment, I don the half-smile. As mentioned previously, I have given myself the lofty goals of continuously being anchored in the present moment and having present-moment awareness. These are the main foci of my spiritual practice and I attempt to apply this practice to as many waking moments throughout the day as possible. There are not nearly as many of these moments as I would like, so I will continue to practice. The half-smile, because it has become the inseparable companion to the present moment, has joined me in these lofty goals. I try to remember to half-smile no matter where I am and no matter what I am doing. Any time I am aware of the present moment, I am half-smiling. Regardless of how many times I forget or fall short, those times I've incorporated the half-smile have vastly improved the quality of my life. I live much more at ease. My demeanor is much more relaxed, pleasant, and softer, and others find me more approachable. Strangers feel comfortable enough around me to strike up conversations. Friends gravitate more toward me and feel safe enough to confide in me. All this from one who's been told many times in the past that he's "very unapproachable." I experience greater love, greater joy, greater compassion, and a greater sense of fulfillment. I find it much easier to accept whatever is in the moment, even if the moment may contain something I might deem unpleasant. Not judging what is in the moment is an entirely different subject that may or may not be broached later on, but even when I do judge, the half-smile still makes it easier to accept.

This small and seemingly insignificant yet immensely powerful and transformative spiritual tool is a game-changer. I highly recommend you give it a try. What is the worst that can happen? Maybe the quality of your life will improve. Maybe it will help you be more mindful. Maybe you will experience present moment awareness. Maybe you will find joy and a lightheartedness you have rarely or perhaps never experienced. You deserve all of these things and more, so give it a chance. Give yourself a chance.

Six Months to the Day

T ime is a funny thing. More accurately, perception of time is a funny thing. Take the last six months of my life, for example. In the grand scheme of things, it might seem a short, insignificant amount of time, but only to the untrained eye. The untrained eye would tell you that I look the same or that I have not lost or gained any weight. It would point out that I have the same job, the same friends, and, for the most part, I follow the same routine. To the untrained eye, it would indeed seem that not much has changed. Yet, to someone who knows, that same six-month period would seem like a lifetime, even an entirely different life altogether. A drastic internal shift has taken place and, along with it, many subtle but significant external changes have occurred.

It has been six months to the day since my awakening. I want to take this moment to look back and take stock of how my life has been transformed as a result of that monumental shift in consciousness and perception. First and foremost, words cannot truly express the immense, sometimes overwhelming gratitude I feel. Gratitude for having been given this gift, for having been brought home, for having been re-introduced to my true self, and for having been freed from the false self that I had long believed was me. Perception being what it is, even though these six months have passed, it is as if the awakening has just happened. I am still completely awestruck and humbled by it. If freedom from the mind and all of its lies, deceptions, and distractions was the only gift I received from this, it would have been more than enough. Knowing the truth is itself a blessing, but there is so much more. I also want to preface this by saying that anything I am sharing with you is to the best of my present ability. As I am fairly new to this, I still have much to learn and will inevitably fall short at times. Also, all of this is subject to change at a moment's notice because the undisciplined mind is still alive and well. If I give it the attention it desires and craves, I can easily be pulled out of the moment and back into its insanity. Thankfully though, because of what I have experienced, because I am aware of the truth because I know what is real and what is not, its distractions no longer have the power over me they once had. Most of the time, I can see them for what they are rather quickly. I can then let go of them and return to the moment. This clarity is another gift I am grateful for.

Speaking of the moment, present-moment awareness has become the main focus in my life, right behind staying clean, of course. As a person in recovery, staying clean must always come first, but living in the moment means living in reality. It means freedom from the illusions of past and future, as well as freedom from fantasies and projected scenarios that may or may not ever manifest. In the here and now, these do not exist. I try to spend every moment being present, to nurture and develop the habit, so that being present becomes second nature. I accomplish this primarily by practicing conscious breathing which anchors me to the here and now. I then bring that presence into my everyday activities. When I am making tea or making breakfast, that is all I am focused on. All of my attention is on that one activity. When I am working, driving, eating, writing, or doing chores, I am focused only on the current task. This keeps me grounded in the present moment and transforms these otherwise ordinary or even mundane activities into meditative practices that enhance my ability to remain present and free. This presence has also improved my ability to listen when in conversation with others. I can listen intently, giving them the space to share their thoughts and feelings, rather than thinking about how I am going to respond or thinking about something else entirely. This improved ability has, in turn, deepened my relationships, for people notice when they receive undivided attention. This gentle acknowledgment of them makes them feel loved and lets them know they are cared for and valued.

For the most part, I still feel no fear, no worry, no anxiety, no regret, no doubt, nor any of the insecurities or negativity that once plagued me. The connection to the Source is ever-present. I feel it in the living flame of love dwelling always in my heart. I take great joy in the simplest of things: the flow of breath in my lungs, the current of life energy that courses through my body, the warmth of sunlight, a cool wind blowing across my face on a warm day, trees slowly waving back and forth in the breeze, even the simple yet profound beauty of a flower. Every joyous observation enhances that connection, fans that loving flame, and teaches me the principles of surrender, acceptance, and stillness. The smile of a stranger reminds me that the love flowing through me has softened me, making me approachable and pleasant to be around. I desire little from the world other than the opportunity to spend time with others and share with them that ever-flowing love. The connection with everyone that I had realized during my transformation has grown so that I can now understand others more deeply. I understand why people do what they do, I understand the reasons behind their actions and I understand their suffering. This is both the cause and the result of the compassion I feel. The compassion allows me to see beyond the surface, to see their suffering, and seeing their suffering breeds even more compassion and more understanding.

I have often said jokingly that the twelve-step recovery process I have been living for 30 years is like Spirituality 101, but the fact is, it has given me a solid foundation and simple but effective skills to practice. I have been able to use and apply those skills in the new life I have been living for the past six months. The principles that the twelve-step process has taught me—daily prayer and meditation, surrender, acceptance, present-moment awareness, love, empathy, compassion, and selfless service—all complement and support this new life. Through them, I have been able to develop a daily regimen of spiritual practices that help keep me grounded and have helped me to establish roots. The consistent application of these tools and principles has deepened my understanding of what I experienced in my awakening and has enabled me to make use of that knowledge in everyday life. Conversely, what I have learned from my awakening and this new life has streamlined my recovery process as well. When turning something over, the trust and faith I have in the constant connection with the Source allow me to feel an immediate sense of letting go and of relief from a burden being lifted. When a character defect pops up, the present moment awareness I have gained enables me to see it immediately, to take pause, and ask for its removal right then and there. Again, I usually feel that immediate sense of relief from it being removed. That same awareness helps me when I make a mistake or commit wrongdoing. I see it right there at that moment and can acknowledge my part honestly, without ego-based justification or rationalization. I can then promptly make any necessary corrections or amends. This frees me from creating any more unnecessary baggage. The clarity and stillness I have gained along with the constant connection to the Source I experience have enhanced my prayers and deepened my meditation in ways I never dreamed possible. And finally, the love, compassion, and gratitude I constantly feel fan the flame of desire to share this gift I have been given, to show others what I have learned. I want to give freely and selflessly that which has been given to me. For I know that this, along with my daily spiritual practice, is what keeps this awakening alive and thriving

The Subject-Object Relationship

I t is said that enlightenment is always enlightenment about something. In my first experience, described in the chapter Transformation, the enlightenment was about who I truly am, about the realization of my true self. During that experience, the false self and false beliefs were simply washed away, leaving behind only the witnessing presence. The false self that I had believed was me was a limited, distorted perception created by the mind in the absence of an understanding of my true self. I would now like to share with you my latest enlightening experience.

I had a wonderful conversation the other night with an individual who had been graced with his own enlightening experience. A friend of mine had given him the Transformation chapter to read. He reached out to me to connect and to talk about my experience, as well as share with me his own. It was a beautiful conversation during which, he sent me a link to Sri Nisargadatta Maharaj's book *I am That.* He also pointed me to a video of Jack Kornfield talking about his experience with Maharaj and some of his teachings. In the video, the subject-object relationship was not explicitly mentioned, but what they both talked about was just that. The information in that video, as well as the first few chapters in the book that I read, weaved their way into meditation the next morning and helped to bring about new enlightenment, a new realization. I will now do my best to try to describe it to you, with the caveat that you already know my feelings about using words to describe spiritual experiences.

As the observing presence, that which the witnessing happens to, I am the subject. The things I witness are the objects. That is the structure of the relationship. The objects witnessed—the events, perceptions, sensations, thoughts, feelings, mental formations, and external stimuli—are ever-changing. I, as presence, am not. I am the constant. The changeless background upon which the ever-changing is perceived. The Maharaj book lays out a process of elimination through negation, through the refusal and release of what is not us, by which the sense of "*I am*," which is the witnessing presence, can be realized. Doing so brings us to the core of the subject–object relationship. Once this point is reached and all the objects have been let go of and fall away, the identification as the witness becomes no longer necessary. It too falls away, and we remain as the awareness. What is a subject without an object to witness? It simply ceases to be. The video addresses the point where you can turn the witness on itself and see nothing is there, that no one is there witnessing, that witnessing "arises like the sun," and that one just sees space and emptiness. I believe this is for two reasons. One is because the subject cannot be the object. The subject is the subject only as it is related to the object it is witnessing or perceiving. With no object, as I have mentioned, the subject is unnecessary and ceases to be. The subject "arises" only if and when there are objects to witness. The other reason the witness disappears is that when the witness turns on itself, it is then looking at the space from which the witness has emerged: the seat of awareness, the home of the Source, the unmanifested space from which all things manifest. It is nothing that can be perceived for it is the very source of perception.

This subject-object relationship is where I had my realization, my enlightenment: in the relationship between me and all that is witnessed. What is not mentioned in the video is my realization that if you turn the witness back around, the entire manifestation reappears in an instant because the subject is once again there to perceive it. From that seat of awareness, all things are manifested, and consciousness is the space in which they manifest as well as the lens through which the witnessing takes place. This is the relationship: no object can exist without a subject to witness it, and no subject or witness can exist without objects to witness. They are partners in the relationship. Both are components of the witnessing that takes place. Interdependence reigns. I am in everything, and everything is in me. All is connected. The idea of separation, along with the ego identity that fuels it, is an illusion created by the mind. In this realization of interdependence, tremendous love is experienced and felt. How can I love myself and not love you? It is impossible, for I am you, and you are me. Towards the end of the video, Kornfield mentions that Maharaj speaks of wisdom and love. "When I see I am nothing, that is wisdom, when I see I am everything, that is love." To me, this speaks directly to the relationship. Without the subject-object relationship, I am nothing. With it, I am everything, and everything is me. I am everyone, and everyone is me.

This realization left me once again in awe and humbled, with a heart full and overflowing with love. I arose from meditation with that fire roaring in my heart and absolutely in tune with the connection to everything and everyone. I was left with the same blissful, joyful, excited sensation I had felt with the previous experience. The circumstances of life have once again taken a back seat, merely a game to be played out. This awareness, this connection, the Oneness has taken the spotlight and has become the main focus. Along with it, there is an abundance of love, joy, compassion, empathy, excitement, playfulness, and smiles.

It was a beautiful day today. There was a brilliant, blue sky with puffy, white clouds floating by in it. While stopped at a red light, I looked up and noticed the clouds slowly drifting through the sky. At that moment, I recalled that I had read in one of Thich Nhat Hanh's Dharma talks about how wonderful it is to experience being a cloud, that he had enjoyed it very much. I looked up at a particular cloud and, for an instant, felt the sensation of slowly, peacefully drifting through the sky. It was so calming and relaxing, and I knew at that moment why he had enjoyed it so much. On occasion, I have also had the experience of being a tree. There was a decent wind today, so the leaves and branches of the trees were blowing back and forth in the breeze. Yet, the trunk and the roots remained still, solid, and peaceful. When I looked at the leaves and branches swaying back and forth, I felt the sensation of swaying back and forth with them. It was a sensation of being at ease and accepting whatever direction the wind blows. At the same time, when I brought my attention down to the trunk and the roots, my body, legs, and feet became still, stable, and very much at peace. I couldn't even stay angry or annoyed with anyone for more than a second or two before realizing that they are me and I am them: that if I am angry with them, I am angry with myself. Seeing as I have no desire to be angry with myself, only to love myself as well as everyone else, in that instant, the anger or annoyance simply melted away.

Of course, along with the love, joy, and bliss of this realization comes the reality that no spiritual awakening can survive for long without regular spiritual maintenance. Maintenance ensures that the mind does not pull my attention into one of its many delusions or distractions. I have some experience with this and know well the tendency to wander off course. So I remain diligent and vigilant in my practice of meditation, mindfulness, present-moment awareness, and acceptance: expressing loving-kindness, compassion, and joy while sharing with others the gifts and realizations I have been blessed to receive.

The Seat of Awareness

I wanted to share another experience, another point of enlightenment, another realization I was graced with shortly after the one about the subject–object relationship. This new realization was inspired by that realization. As previously stated, enlightenment is always enlightenment about something. In this case, it is enlightenment about the seat of awareness, about the Source.

I have noticed that since the initial experience, there has been a constant connection to the Source. I am referring to the ever-present feeling of love, that never-ending flame in the heart which I have spoken of many times. I have often wondered why this is so. Yes, it is true that the constant practice I have been engaged in since that experience helps keep me from getting distracted by the mind and keeps my attention in the present. For it is only in the present that the connection can be felt. However, I felt that there had to be more to it than just that.

It was early morning and I had just settled in for my meditation when this realization struck me. What I realized is that the very idea of having had this experience is itself a mental formation, only a memory. I also realized that the perception that I had been to the place where the Source resides, sat with it, merged with it, became one with it, experienced all of existence as the Source, and then returned to my body is nothing more than the mind's attempt to reconcile something that is beyond its capabilities for, as I have mentioned, this experience was beyond the mind. I realized that the connection I feel is constant because I never left that seat of awareness. I never left because I never went in the first place. It is not a place to go to and leave, it is the place where I always am, and I was simply unaware. It is the core of my very existence. What happened during that awakening experience is that the distorted perception or distorted sense of self that had obscured my ability to see the truth, to see reality, was stripped away. The blocks were removed, the veil was pulled back, and I could finally see clearly. This seat of awareness, the Source behind all manifestations, behind all objects that exist, behind even consciousness itself, is where I truly reside. It is my home. It always has been and always will be: as if past and future were anything more than just concepts themselves. It is from this seat that I see, that I witness, that I am aware of all that is: for I am that awareness. It is my true nature.

I realize that the last statement can sound narcissistic or even megalomaniacal, but only if one is perceiving from an individual perspective, which is the case for those who are still identified with their physical form. Separation only appears to exist in that limited physical sense. In reality, there is no such thing. I am not saying that I, as an individual, am the Source. I am saying that *all* is the Source or rather, the Source is that from which everything has appeared. At the Source, there is no separation, no distinction.

That distinction melted away and ceased to be in the previous chapter when all other objects had been released and the need for a subject, for the "I am" was no longer necessary. I am speaking of Oneness, of the connection between all of us and all that is. The Source is that common seed from which all has sprouted.

This realization has merely solidified that feeling of connection I first felt during the initial experience. It has deepened and made much clearer my understanding of that experience. It is not merely an idea or a concept to contemplate, it is something of which I am firmly aware with certitude, with conviction. It is concrete, it is reality. When this eye-opening realization struck me, tears streamed down my face and my heart swelled with love. It was as if someone had flipped a switch and I was once again bathed in light just as I had been during that initial experience. At that moment, I felt a whisper utter the words, "You got it! Welcome home!"

The World,
As We Know It

Perception is everything in terms of how we experience the world around us. Our ability to perceive things is what shapes reality for us. Yet, for most of us, this realization is taken for granted. For those who have use of their eyes, the way they see things, the way things look to them, is mostly ignored. It is an automatic thing. For those who have lost their eyesight, the loss of their ability is a harsh reality. They can see the way things look only through memory. Anything new they cannot see at all. For those who were born blind, the way things look does not even exist. It is not a part of reality as they experience it. The same can be said of a man who can hear versus a man who is deaf. So it is our perception that determines our experience of life and the world.

If you were to take two different people and ask them the question, "How's life?" you might be surprised at the variance in their responses. One might say, "Life is beautiful!" whereas the other might declare, "Life Sucks!" How, from such a simple question, could you receive such drastically different answers?

Which one would be right? Well, both are right, of course, because our perception of life and the world is not only filtered through our senses but also through our experiences, our opinions, our beliefs, our conditioning, through everything we have been taught. If we look at a car, for the most part, we will all agree that it is a car. You get in it and drive it from place to place. It is a mode of transportation. But what if someone were told their whole life that what we know as a car was a boat? To them, calling it a car would be incorrect and downright absurd. Again, who would be right? Both of them.

This difference in perception and opinion is the basis for all of the discrimination, racism, and bigotry that exists in the world. It is also responsible for most of the conflict, hatred, and violence as well. Every war that has ever taken place has been fought over a difference of opinion and perception because one person or group of people was convinced that their group was right whereas the other one was wrong. If people were to realize that when it comes to perception, there is no right or wrong, that it is all subjective, all of that would cease. The truth is that no one sees the world as it is. We see it as we are. The very idea of an "as it is" is invalid because the world can be experienced only through our perception.

The ego perceives in the absence of knowledge of our true selves. Due to its attachment to and identification with the body, it perceives us as separate and different from everyone and everything else. It needs to have that sense of uniqueness to fuel itself. It craves separation, judgment, opposition, conflict, drama, superiority, and inferiority. It doesn't matter which side of an argument we take, so long as a mental position is established against someone or something. If challenged, the ego becomes even more entrenched in its position. It feeds off the negative energy generated by these perceptions, false as they may be. If no conflict exists, it will try to create one. It is an entire identity that has taken the place of who we truly are. It convinces us that it is real by generating thoughts and feelings, usually focused on the past or future, that provide evidence of its authenticity. But this identity, this false self-image, is as flawed, fragile, and as impermanent as the body that it clings to. It is merely that: an image. It is a limited, distorted perception of our true selves. As a result of this diminished sense of self, we suffer from fear, insecurity, doubt, worry, and feelings of incompleteness or insufficiency. Our perception of reality becomes blurred, skewed, and warped because it is filtered through all of this falseness and negativity. We wind up viewing the world and those in it as hostile, threatening, and dangerous. We become selfish and obsessive, with an incessant need to take and to consume because of our fear that we will not have what we need or that what we have will be taken away.

Many live their entire lives like this: duped by their ego, stuck in false and warped perceptions of reality. I too have spent much of my life in such a state. There was no love, no connection with others, nor a proper sense of proportion with relation to the world. The energy of such things is positive and vibrates at a much higher frequency than the ego does, so these things are incompatible with it. I rejected them because they seemed foreign and threatening. All that existed for me was fear and an overwhelming sense of loneliness and isolation. To wake me up, it took the intense pain and suffering of a life lived in isolation, fear, and repercussions from the actions I had taken to avoid those feelings. Once awakened, I rediscovered my true nature and was freed from the false self and all that went along with it. Evolution, although a natural phenomenon, is almost always forced. Nothing nor no one voluntarily goes through the process. It takes place out of necessity. Circumstances arise that compel adaptation from the way something or someone currently exists. Change occurs, or that someone or something dies due to its inability to adapt. So, in a sense, I have evolved. My lenses have been cleared. The veil of obscurity created by the false self and all of its false perceptions has been peeled back. I can now see what is real.

This dramatic shift in perception, this realization of the true self, has raised my vibrational frequency to that of those things I mentioned earlier: love, connection, Oneness, the reality that exists in the here and now. These are the things I now perceive, feel, and experience in the world. To me, the world is now seen as a loving, beautiful place full of miracles. It is filled with people to connect with, share with, and love. Those things exuding negative energy and a lower frequency are no longer palpable. They still exist, but they no longer resonate with me. The ego is all but non-existent although, so long as the body exists, the potential for it to reassert itself remains. This generally only happens when I am tired or emotional, as these conditions tend to cloud my vision. When it does reassert itself, it no longer has the same power or influence it once did. I usually recognize it quickly and know that it is false. I no longer suffer the tunnel vision of obsession. This is a most wonderful benefit of having a clear vision. I sit way, way back behind all the objects I perceive in the world, behind the world itself, behind the consciousness in which all objects manifest, all the way back in the seat of awareness. From here I am afforded a most widespread, inclusive view.

I attempt to share this view with others, for I am no longer consumed with selfishness and the need to take. I offer freely the gift of awareness that has been given me. I offer it to those who are drawn to me, though not all can see. Some do not yet have the eyes to see such a wide-open view. Their lenses are still fogged, and the veil of falsehood still obscures their vision. Some do though, and I welcome them home with open arms and love. I also realize that, even while perceiving reality instead of falsehood, things are going to be perceived through the unique lens of our own experiences. Thus, each of us will have a unique interpretation. The difference now is in the realization that the basic building blocks are the same. We focus on similarities rather than differences. We live in harmony, rather than in opposition, and we can seek to connect on common ground, rather than seeking to separate by focusing on variances based on interpretation. This is the world in which I live, the world I perceive, the world, as I know it.

Breaking the Habit

Such habitual creatures we are. Through repetition of actions and behaviors, we form habits. We perform mundane tasks and routines almost automatically, with little or no thought involved. Day after day we get up, eat, drink, shower, brush our teeth, cook or order our meals, go to work, clean the dishes, do the laundry, watch television, and go to sleep. We do all this without much thought or effort, as simple as breathing. One could say a large portion of life is lived on autopilot.

Most habits such as these are harmless and can provide us with a sense of structure, stability, and comfort. In doing so they are good and healthy for us. There are also habits born of abuse, negative conditioning, reinforcement, neglect, or simply unconscious urges. Habits such as these are born in the absence of awareness of our true selves. They have their roots in fear and its subsequent manifestations. They are destructive, causing pain and suffering to ourselves and all those concerned with our lives. Unhealthy habits that many of us suffer from include substance abuse; physical or mental abuse to ourselves and/or others;

obsessive, negative, or critical thinking; negative self-talk, putting ourselves down; overeating, and other compulsive behaviors; even choosing unhealthy friends or relationship partners over and over again. Some of these habits are so old and so deeply ingrained that we are not even aware they exist. We just seem to suffer endlessly and do not understand why. Even when we are aware of these habits and put forth great effort to stop or change them, we falter and fall back because these habits have become a part of who we believe we are. Having learned many of them long ago, growing up in the only formative environment available to us, these habits have physically imprinted on the neural pathways in our brains. Even if they are destructive, they can feel normal and comfortable. To try to change them feels wrong as if we are "going against the grain." As I have mentioned, such habits carry with them momentum from years of activity and use. They drag us along even when we no longer want them to.

So what are we to do? Suffer endlessly from the torment of these habits? Live lives of misery and frustration? So many of us have and do. I did for many years. Even now, despite all I have learned, realized, and experienced, despite all the growing and changing that has taken place, there are still some habits that resurface from time to time. Thus the need for this chapter. It is as much for me as it is for you. Should we fight and struggle against our brain design and chemistry, against years of conditioning, constantly pushing ourselves uncomfortably against that grain while trying to break these habits? We can, and we might succeed in some cases. Habits are formed through repetition, and repetition can break them. The deeper and older the habit though, the longer it will take to break it, and the more consistent and persistent our efforts will have to be to accomplish this. Just know that these habits have had one hell of a head start. In most cases, we simply do not have the stamina or drive to undertake such an endeavor. I think if we did, such habits would not have formed in the first place. I am not trying to sound defeatist or negative. Perhaps there is another way.

Rather than focusing on the external conditions and actions that have formed and also reinforce these habits, we can use the powers of investigation and introspection to look deeply into the internal factors. We can use our luminous nature to shine light into the darkness, revealing the conditions that were present within us at the time such habits were formed. I am referring to that sense of living on autopilot. Living a life of resignation, passivity, and sloth has allowed the creation and solidification of these habits. This may have been the result of poor guidance or of the negative reinforcement I mentioned earlier, which damaged our self-esteem and left us believing we were incapable of much else. Also mentioned earlier, was the lack of awareness of our true selves. This ignorance allowed the ego, the false self, to take hold and run our lives. Any perceptions or beliefs born of such a fragile, false entity are bound to be as unhealthy and destructive as the ego itself. We are not the ego. We are not the false self-image created through ignorance. We are the one who sees, who watches all of these things as they arise and operate. Realize this, and you will begin to take your life back.

I believe what is needed more than anything else to solve this problem is attention. An active sense of awareness diligently and consistently applied to watching our mind, our thoughts, and our destructive habits will allow them to dissolve on their own.

This awareness is our luminous nature. These habits develop, grow, and thrive in the darkness of our apathy. With the light of awareness and truth shining on them, they can no longer hide and flourish in the darkness of an unaware mind. Give them no place to call home, and these habits will go away. In many cases, not much more effort than that is required. Simply live a life of active awareness instead of a life of resignation, and watch what happens.

Still, though, some habits may persist. As I mentioned before, even with all of my awareness, all of my realizations, and understanding, some habits resurface from time to time. Granted, they do not have the power and influence over me they once had, but they do persist. Rather than trying to alter neural pathways that are so deeply carved, why not simply make new ones? I have been creating new, healthy habits based on active awareness, rather than in resignation. These habits include conscious breathing, meditation, mindfulness in my daily activities, and the aforementioned half-smile. Even the most mundane activity becomes a spiritual practice when I am mindful and half-smiling, even when I might not want to. This does not mean masking or denying my true feelings or being false and deceitful. However, smiling as a practice can often change the way I feel. It is an effective spiritual tool.

Creating new habits is much easier than breaking old ones. Once new habits are in place, we then have a choice. We can simply choose the new, healthier habits and let the old, destructive ones gradually dissolve through inactivity. No doubt this is a process that takes diligent practice. However, as our active awareness grows and develops, it will help us to acknowledge the old habits as destructive and the new ones as constructive, making the choice easier. Freedom from our habits is possible, but it requires a shift in our fundamental understanding of who we are as well as a shift in how we live. Once the truth is known, autopilot is no longer an acceptable way to live. A life of active awareness and right action will grant us the liberation from these destructive habits that we so desperately desire. It will allow us to change, to grow, to heal, and to be free.

Facing Death

In light of the death of my dear friend Paul this week, one who had been traveling this journey with me, I feel it necessary to talk about facing death. As I sit here writing, I sit with a heaviness of heart, with sadness, and with grief. The body experiences these feelings as a response to the vacuity left behind by Paul's physical absence. There is also a sense of despondency in the realization that no new memories are to be formed with him, no new experiences to be shared. Still, it is not all I feel. I also feel tremendous joy and love, both for him and for life itself. I am thankful for being alive, for breathing in and out, for feeling the flow of energy in my body, for seeing, hearing, and smelling the world around me with my eyes, ears, and nose, for being able to touch all that exists in this physical world. Sadness and joy can co-exist, and it is perfectly natural to feel both at the same time. I recall memories of the time we've spent together: of laughs we've shared, of happiness we've enjoyed, of difficulties and struggles we helped carry each other through, of sadness and pain we've endured. I cherish them all, and when I bring him into the mind and heart like that, he lives on in me.

Our society and many other cultures shy away from death. They seek to hide it, to avoid it, many even fear it. But by giving our lives a limited duration, death gives life meaning and makes it something to cherish. It is the contrast that gives life its color. As Eckhart says, if blue were the only color that existed and everything were blue, we would not know what blue is. A contrast, something that is not blue, is needed for us to know what blue is, for it to convey meaning and significance. Death provides that contrast. To avoid, to shy away from, or to hide death takes away from the value and beauty of life. To face death head-on and appreciate it for the richness it gives to life is to truly embrace life. Doing so allows us to live a deep and meaningful existence. Embracing mortality reminds us to take nothing for granted, for our time here is short. It allows us to appreciate every moment and to find gratitude for the simplest of things. This is the type of life I live. I hold near and dear to my heart everything and everyone that touches my life. I know the temporary nature of this existence but I do not fear it, for I have met death, faced it head-on, and welcomed it as a friend. Even with grief and sadness in my heart, I smile because I know the benefits death gives to life.

Attending the wake was an absolute privilege. I had the opportunity to be fully present and to embrace the moment as it was. Even with sadness, grief, and loss within me and all around me, I still felt love and joy. I was able to be there for so many others: for family, for friends, for all who came to pay their respects or to say goodbye. I held so many people in my arms, cried with them, and let the love that comes from deep within pour through me to help soothe the pain and suffering in their aching hearts. While we shared stories and memories, I had the chance to share with many of them what I have come to realize: that death is not an end. It is a transformation, a transition, simply a dissolving of the physical form. It is not an end because we are not these bodies. They are a temporary physical manifestation, a temporary housing, which allows us to experience human existence. We are the life energy that flows through the body, animating it, as well as the luminous presence that witnesses all there is and all that takes place. Without us, the body is nothing more than a lifeless shell. I realize, though, that not all see what I see and know what I know. Those who do not see and do not know as I do suffer the pain of the physical loss because they know little or nothing beyond the body. I feel the sadness and heaviness in my body, but I do not suffer it. I simply allow the feelings to be, as I watch with loving affection and peace. Being graced with the opportunity to be there for others, to be still and solid so that they can lean on me while at their weakest, is the absolute privilege I mentioned earlier. It is one of my highest aspirations to be able to care for others, to be able to support them in times of need, to love them, to nurture them, and to share with them what I've learned so that maybe they can come to know it themselves. I am profoundly grateful whenever such opportunities arise.

I have come to realize that the body, as well as the world we perceive, is merely a projection of our inner Self. I believe it is why Gandhi advised being the change we want to see in the world. He knew that if we changed ourselves, then the world we perceived, the projection, would change as a result. The manifestation of the world and our bodies allows us to experience human existence, to play the game of life. Our body is our character in the game, and the game seems very real. So much so, that for generations we have believed it to be reality. This mistaken belief is the source of our suffering. Because of our attachment to these temporary manifestations, we suffer birth and death, we suffer fear, need, longing, and we suffer from desires that can never truly be fulfilled. Such desires, after all, are based in an impermanent world, so any fulfillment of them will only ever be temporary. Our true self and our true home reposes behind all of these transient objects of perception. This home is the seat of awareness. This physical playground is only where the game of life is played. At any time, we can turn our attention away from it and back towards our home. When we do, our eternal nature is revealed, and attachment to that which is temporary ends, as does our suffering. Then this game of life is a joy to play when we play it.

Without this realization, we suffer from the experience of death. I say again, death is not an end. The only thing that ends is our opportunity to play the game with our current character. When the death of the body occurs, the consciousness which inhabited the body returns home. That character no longer has a role to play in the game. Do we eventually receive another character and another chance to play the game? Who is to say? Memories are stored in the brain, which dissolves with the body, so I do not recall if I have played the game before as another character or not. It is possible, for although I have no memories of past lives, I do have a sense of wisdom about things and an indescribable and inexplicable familiarity with things. I do not concern myself with such questions, though, because questions that have no answer are nothing more than distractions. They offer little or no relevance to the here and now.

In realizing our true self, we can "die" to this world every day and return our attention to our true home, freeing ourselves of the illusion that this game of life is reality. We do not need to die physically for this to be. We need only to realize what we are and what we are not. And when death eventually comes for the body, we will have nothing to fear because we will know that we never really die. Rest easy my friend. Good game and welcome home.

The Cinema

Going to the movies is a wonderful, enjoyable, fun experience. We go to the theater, get our popcorn, our snacks, our drinks, and we go in to find a seat. But where to sit? This is important because if we sit too close to the screen we will not get a good view of the movie. We will have only a limited perception of what is happening onscreen. We know that the farther back we sit, the wider the scope, and the more expansive the cinematic experience we will be. We don't want to miss a thing, so we move deeper and farther back into the theater. If we go all the way to the back, we will see the whole screen and even have much of the theater itself in our scope. Now, this may not seem appealing when going to see a movie, because the goal is to become immersed in the movie and lose our awareness that we are sitting in the theater altogether. We want to sink in and become a part of the movie. We want to feel what the characters are feeling. We want to laugh with them, we want to cry with them, we want to be angry with them, we want to struggle with them in overcoming adversity, we want to be on the edge of our seat in nervousness, excitement, and anticipation when the action is intense, hanging on every moment as it unfolds and plays out. This makes for a good movie experience when the movie is so engaging that we lose ourselves in it.

But what of the movie we come to see every day: the one we watch play out from the time we wake until the time we sleep? I am speaking, of course, of the movie of life. When we come to watch this movie, to witness life unfolding, it is truly engaging, for we are not just the audience coming to watch and witness, but we are also the star of the film. All that takes place in the movie and unfolds before us we experience first-hand. All of the events that occur, all of the emotions and thoughts that arise, all the highs and lows, every bit of it we live as it unfolds.

It is effortless to become immersed in the movie of life, to lose ourselves in it. Some spend their whole lives lost in it, unaware that they are the audience as well as the star, that they are the witness of life unfolding. While seeing this movie, being in this theater, it is best to do as I've mentioned before: to go as deep in and as far back as we can in the theater so that we can not only take in the whole film but so far back that we can also be aware of the theater itself, aware of the field of consciousness. This will prevent us from losing ourselves in the movie. We can watch it, seeing all that transpires as it unfolds, and still be the witness of all that comes before us.

There remains one space I've yet to mention, one space further back and deeper in than even the very last seat in the theater, for even that very last seat is still within the theater, still within the field of consciousness. The space I speak of is the projection booth from whence the movie originates and emanates. Beyond the theater, beyond the field of consciousness lies the source from where the movie manifests. In that space lies the film, the very elements that constitute life as well as the light of the projector. Without that light, the movie would not exist. It is the shining of that light through the film that creates the images that are projected into the field of consciousness, into the theater, and onto the screen for us to witness. In the projection booth, at the source, we are the light of the projector. We are the light of awareness, which shines through those elements, bringing the film to life.

From this seat in the projection booth, from the source where the movie of life manifests, through our luminous awareness, we can see the projection of images into the theater and onto the screen, and we can watch the movie of life play out, with our manifest selves as the star at the center of the movie. The screen, like the moment, captures the images of the movie, and although the events of the movie pass before it, like the moment, the screen remains unchanged and unaffected by them. It is the constant beyond the concepts of space and time in which the events appear to take place. From the booth, we can also see the theater itself, the field of consciousness. Within it, we can see our Self as the witness watching the movie. As well, we can see the popcorn, the drinks, all of the objects of consciousness that manifest within that field. We can see our Self as all of these things because, when perceived from the source, these things are all one within the totality of consciousness. There is no separation. There also is no "we." There is only the Unmanifested, as Eckhart Tolle calls it, or the Absolute, as Sri Nisargadatta Maharaj called it. When all of the illusions, stories, and identifications of who you believe yourself to be eventually melt away, and you revert to that Unmanifested, Absolute state, it becomes clear that all of these perceived differences are only a matter of appearance. The Self becomes synonymous with all. The movie, the audience, the snacks, the entire theater, and all it contains are seen as one. You can still enjoy the movie, but you no longer get lost in it because you know your true Self. You know the movie to be just a part of the greater whole. Indeed, you come to love the movie all the more because you understand it to be a part of you. As the realization of the Self becomes the realization of all, the Self-love becomes the love of all, including the movie of life.

Holiday Cheer

I t is Christmas morning and I want to wish a Merry Christmas to those of you who celebrate. I arose from meditation this morning with a heart full of love and joy. A Christmas miracle has occurred. For the first time, I feel that there is room in my heart for everyone. This has been a goal of mine since the day of my awakening, and it is through diligence and persistence that this moment has arrived. It is the universe's gift to me. The opportunity to share this with you, to invite you into my heart is my gift to you, for giving is one of the truest expressions of love.

Thich Nhat Hanh speaks of the holiday season as a time to return home and to reconnect with family, with our roots. Just as Santa brings a mixed bag of toys for all the children, reflecting on this brings a mixed bag of emotions for me. Last night there were many tears, both of sadness and joy. Sadness because Christmas Eve is when my immediate family would celebrate the holiday. We are of mostly German ancestry, and with my mother having been born and raised in Germany, it has always been our family's tradition, as it is a German tradition to celebrate Christmas Eve. As I sat at home last night, her absence and the absence of that celebration, that time for us to be together, was felt intensely. Mom passed away many years ago. Dad moved away to Virginia and has since remarried. One of my sisters married into a Jewish family, and they don't celebrate Christmas. So there was no feeling of reconnection nor returning to my roots. I felt alone. Ever since Mom passed away, Christmas Eve has been bittersweet, not just for me but for my sisters and Dad as well. The holiday had always been a really big deal for Mom but, in her absence, we all seem to have lost interest in celebrating. Without her here, none of us felt a strong enough desire to carry on the tradition. We would make half-hearted attempts to get together, but it all eventually fell apart.

I did have the good fortune of spending some time with family earlier in the day, though. I even had an opportunity to connect and have a lovely conversation with a cousin I hadn't spoken to in a long time. We spoke of life as it is now as well as reflecting a bit on the past. I was thinking about how he had chosen the outer path—school, career, wife, children, and family— whereas I had chosen the inner path, of spiritual practice, growth, and enlightenment. I thought of how both paths, despite being different, can lead to a satisfying life complete with a sense of fulfillment. Yet, despite that wonderful time together and the joy that was felt in being with family during the holiday, later on, I felt that absence and that sadness, so it was a bit of a roller coaster of emotions. Even amidst the sadness, though, there was joy, because I know my mother lives on through me. I see so much of her in me and I know she is never truly gone.

There is also much gratitude for the simple fact that these emotions are even present and that I am present to feel them.

Presence is my favorite of all the presents. There were many, many years spent with my heart completely closed off, when the holidays and time with family meant nothing and was often an annoyance or even something to suffer. There were some years when I did not even show up to family gatherings, making up some excuse for why I could not be there. The false self had deluded me into feeling such a sense of separation that I felt completely alien around the people I would have otherwise felt close to and felt a connection with. I felt completely detached from my roots and was convinced that I wanted nothing to do with them. Much of my life had been spent feeling alone, with no one but my mind to keep me company. This, as you might know from previous mentions, was more torment than companionship. Even later on in recovery, after years of being clean when I had already started on my spiritual path, I would come to holiday gatherings out of obligation, in an attempt to make amends for the times I had been absent. These trying times were, of course, all necessary steps on the journey. Pain, being the motivator that it is, propelled me toward awakening so I embrace and honor it, for without it I would not know myself as I do today nor would I know the truth. Upon awakening, all of the lies, illusions, delusions, and falsehoods were stripped away, including that false sense of separation. The feeling of being connected returned. Yesterday, as well as all the other family gatherings that have happened throughout the year, have been occasions to grow closer to the family I had kept at a distance for all of these years: an opportunity to reconnect with my roots.

Last night gave me the chance to purge old sadness, heal some old wounds, and release much of the trapped energy from past experiences that had been buried inside. This, in turn, allowed me to have the morning I have enjoyed. It cleared out that old stuff and made room in my heart for everyone. It made room for a seemingly endless amount of love. I look forward to spending Christmas Day today with family, inviting them into my heart as well. Days such as these are no longer an obligation or a burden, they are a blessing.

Become What You Need

As Hannibal from *The A-Team* used to say, "I love it when a plan comes together." I love it when a series of events unfold that lead to a new realization and understanding about myself, including spiritual and emotional healing and growth.

I have never enjoyed being the center of attention or being in front of a room full of people. I have always felt uncomfortable with public speaking. Before a speaking engagement, my mind constantly tries to rehearse what I'm going to say. Flurries of anxious thoughts pull me away from the present moment, distracting me from the here and now. The reasons for this inner turmoil are obvious: I don't want to embarrass myself, nor do I want to sound bad. Instead, I want to articulate well so that I am understood, and I want to be effective at conveying my thoughts, feelings, and information. The frustration created by that constant mental distraction is what brought about the current realization. For me, the uneasiness goes far beyond these simple, surface reasons. It goes all the way back to second grade.

It was a short while after the incident with my sister's adoption papers and the subsequent fiasco. The trauma of it, as well as the mistrust born from that situation, were still fresh. On this particular day, the feelings of sadness, hurt, and aloneness were too much to bear. They overwhelmed me, resulting in me laying my head down on the desk in class and, as quietly as possible, crying my eyes out uncontrollably for what was probably an hour. No one seemed to notice, for I had made every effort to be silent, as I did not want to draw attention to myself. Even at that young age, emotional outbursts were completely foreign and unacceptable. I did not want to appear to be weak nor did I want to be embarrassed. Perhaps they just figured I was tired or feeling ill and simply paid me no mind. By the end of class, when the other students began to get up to leave, everyone noticed me. One of the students lifted my head, and my cover was pulled. Tears and snot were all over my face and all over the desk from the hour of crying, and all of the other students laughed at me, made fun of me, and ridiculed me. Not only was I traumatized by uncontrollable tears and sadness, but now I had been publicly humiliated. Once the teacher realized what was happening, she rushed the rest of the students out of the class. The wonderful human being that she was, she cleaned me up, comforted and consoled me until the tears finally stopped and I could regain some composure. She never reported this incident to anyone in the school nor my parents, assuming she wanted to spare me from further embarrassment. Like every other traumatic experience I had been through, this was never discussed. It was just swept under the rug and forgotten about. As you can imagine, this experience scarred me, further reinforced the mistrust I already had brewing and made me want to never feel publicly embarrassed or ridiculed again. Thus, my discomfort with public speaking and being in front of a crowd.

The connection between these feelings of discomfort and that traumatic childhood experience was realized only a week ago. One of the "a-ha!" moments, as I like to call them. I discussed this with my dear friend Kaia because I respect and appreciate her opinion and insight. I follow her suggestions far more often than she allows herself to believe. She suggested that I meditate on it and see what else arises. The very next morning I did just that. I used the same technique that enabled me to have the conversation with my mother, which I have spoken about previously: I invited second-grade Danny into the present moment, into the meditation space. I embraced him, comforted him, and let him know that he was not alone. It was soothing and healing, and I cried a bit during the embrace. What I did not know back then but do now is that tears have a cleansing property that helps wash away the pain of emotional wounds and helps prevent them from becoming infected and festering. What happened afterward was unexpected but wonderful. I showed second-grade Danny who he is in the here and now and let him know he is not just the scared, sad, lonely child. I showed him that he is big, strong, and not so easily ridiculed. Comforted and reassured of his nature, I sent young Danny on his way and arose from the meditation feeling as if I had done some good for the inner child.

The next day I reached out to Kaia to report back to her what had transpired. She was, of course, incredibly happy about it, but she inquired, "Did you speak to young Danny? Did you ask him what he wants or needs?" It never dawned on me to do so, because young Danny and present-moment Danny are, in essence, the same only differing in age, experience, and circumstances. I assumed I knew how he felt and what he wanted and needed as a result of the previous day's meditative experience. Nevertheless, open to her suggestions, the very next morning I once again brought young Danny into the moment in meditation and spoke with him. I asked him what he needed, what he wanted, what he longed for. He said "I don't ever want to feel this way again. I also do not want to feel like I am all alone. I want someone I can trust, someone I can look up to and feel safe and ok with. Someone who will always be honest with me. I think and feel a lot of things that I do not always understand, but I feel as if I do not have anyone I can talk to about them. So I want someone I can talk to when I'm feeling stuff, someone who will pay attention, and someone I can ask questions of when I'm not sure or don't know what to do." As I paid attention and listened to him, I was struck with the realization that present-moment Danny is the embodiment of all the things that young Danny wanted and needed. He is honest, compassionate, and caring. He listens to and pays attention to those who speak with him or come to him seeking advice or guidance, and he shares with them openly and honestly what he knows, seeking only to help. He is consistent and stable, dependable, always there when needed. He is not afraid of feeling whatever arises, and he is not afraid of others hurting him. He understands that people who hurt others do so because of their hurt, unskillfully dealt with, and transmitted as a result of their conditioning. In those instances, he tries to understand, to be compassionate, and to help if it is possible to do so. At the very least he tries not to react and create more hurt. I realized at that moment that he had become the very person that child had longed for. In doing so, he was able to provide the child with the help and healing that was needed. I also realized, at that moment, that young Danny's desires and needs had been a driving force throughout his life. They had driven him to become the person he is today. I was overjoyed with this new awareness and let the child know that I would always be there for him, would always be the person he needed, and would always be there whenever he needed me. I once again sent him on his way and arose from meditation feeling as if I had begun healing a very deep and ancient wound.

Since having this experience, I feel that the mind's desire to rehearse has weakened and no longer carries with it the influential power it once had. I also feel that, as time goes on, this desire will continue to diminish and will likely dissolve altogether. I believe the awkwardness and discomfort of being in front of a crowd, of public speaking, will also diminish. I will have the opportunity to test this theory, as I have a speaking engagement coming up shortly.

The realization and awareness that I have become what I need to heal is a gift beyond measure, one that will truly be significant as life continues to unfold. I also do not think it is something exclusive. I believe everyone can become what they need. I encourage you all to love yourself enough to do so. Embrace your hurt, embrace your wounds, speak to the child within, find out what he or she needs to heal, and become that.

I bet many of you already have but have yet to realize it. If you have not done so, then you owe it to yourself and to that child to try. You deserve to heal and you deserve to have your needs fulfilled. We all do.

How Did I Get Here?

I am not one to dwell too much on the past because the past only exists in the mind and therefore, is not technically real. It is only memory. When it continually and repeatedly presents itself in the present, though, I need to take note of it. It is clear to me that the past is trying to get my attention.

Early childhood keeps coming up in conversations. As I continue to gain clarity and understanding, things from the past are resurfacing, but I am seeing them with new eyes. In particular, I am referring to the unexplainable feeling I have always had that something isn't quite right with the world, that somehow this is not the way things are supposed to be. As a child, that feeling turned inward, and I began to assume there was something wrong with me for feeling that way. It seemed that no one else felt or thought similarly, so I concluded that it must be just me. But it is this feeling that has been coming to light, not the dysfunction that followed, and it is now being viewed through a clear perspective and with deeper understanding.

As disidentification with the body has taken root and my identity as the Self grows clearer, the matter of that vague feeling from childhood has come into focus and has brought about a realization. The physical and emotional distress experienced as a newborn was not nearly as traumatizing as consciousness manifesting and then losing its identity in that physical form. That early childhood feeling stems from the lingering sense of having existed prior to the manifestation of consciousness, coupled with the disorientation of that budding consciousness losing its identity in that body. Of course, that lingering sense can only be alluded to by way of the contrast of the manifest counterpart. Existence prior to consciousness cannot be perceived directly, as there is no apparatus for perceiving it. That Absolute or Unmanifested state can only be reflected in the manifest consciousness. It is through the direct perception of consciousness that we can have an inkling of our existence prior to it because for us to know or perceive anything, including consciousness, we must exist prior to it. Forgive me if this sounds confusing. I am attempting to use words to describe that which is indescribable and unknowable. Words exist within consciousness so they will always fall short when discussing that which is beyond it. The ignorant nature of childhood, the inability to comprehend or articulate, left that lingering sense as the vague, confusing feeling of something not being right. Also, with all that is learned in early childhood, with all of the data and sensory input pouring in and the mind interpreting that data, forming and developing memories and associations, it is no wonder that this budding consciousness latched on to the body. It was the only thing that appeared solid amidst the swirling sea of those thoughts, feelings, perceptions, and information. Given the aforementioned clarity and understanding, that early, vague feeling becomes clear. It was an instinctive or intuitive resistance to identification with the body. This is what seemed and felt wrong. Somehow, even then I knew that this was incorrect. Another factor that only recently came to light is that the pain and trauma suffered as an infant made the body undesirable and unpleasant to identify with, hence that instinctive resistance.

That feeling never quite went away entirely. It manifested in other subtle ways throughout life. As an older child and into adolescence, it manifested as a general sense of uneasiness or discomfort that could not be pinpointed in any particular source. Later on, in adulthood, in recovery, it manifested as a feeling that there had to be more to life than this. Even after decades of recovery, with many trips through the 12-step process and a firm spiritual foundation, there was still this feeling that there had to be something more. Pain as a catalyst also played a huge part as an adult. The constant pain that this body suffered had been coupled with that almost burning need to find out more. This facilitated the awakening and spontaneous break from identification with the body that took place nearly a year ago. I hadn't realized or understood this at the time, but now it is remarkably clear. Had the pain not been persistently present, making identification with the body uncomfortable and unappealing, I do not believe that break would have occurred.

From this realization arise many questions: What the hell happened? How did I get here? What caused this consciousness to manifest, and how did it mistake itself for the body? Was this a choice, and if so, why would I choose to give up the perfect bliss of the Unmanifested for this manifest existence? And, if it was not a choice, what compelled me to do so? Is there some meaning or purpose in being conscious? Keep in mind that all the movements mentioned here—the leaving, coming, arriving, and so on—are not actual movements but shifts of awareness, attention, perception, and focus. Unfortunately, I do not have answers to all of these questions. Answers to some of them may be as unknowable as the Absolute itself because the causes or conditions that lead to consciousness manifesting stem from that unmanifested space. Moreover, there is no single cause. Anything that manifests or any event that takes place has multiple causes and factors. Even if an answer to them were knowable it would not, could not be a simple, clear-cut answer. That being said, given what I have come to understand thus far, I can say that as the body formed and was imbued with life energy, it required a sense of awareness to know that it exists. This awareness is consciousness in seed form and was present during the formation of the body. All manifestation takes place in consciousness, so everything that manifests has within it that seed-consciousness. The life force and consciousness are always present together in the body. All three—consciousness, life energy, and the body—are required for a life form to exist and have sentience. For discussion and clarification, I speak of the three separately. In reality, there is no separation. They are all part of the Manifest Self. As that seed-consciousness began to blossom, it latched onto the body and took it to be its form, providing it with a sense of solidity so as not to be overwhelmed by the flood of sense perceptions and information pouring in. That misidentification was then reinforced by the conditioning from outside sources. In doing so, consciousness was diminished and reduced to the individual level of self-awareness called the ego. This ego is not inherently bad or negative. It is necessary for the development from childhood to adulthood. It allows a sense of individuality and independence to form, helping the maturation process to take place. Once that has occurred, however, if not discarded, the ego becomes a hindrance. Think of it in the same way a cast is used to mend a broken bone. Initially, it is useful and helpful but, at a certain point, the cast is discarded allowing the limb to regain its original stature. Similarly, this individual ego identity formed through the attachment to the body needs to be discarded so that consciousness can regain its infinite, universal stature.

The analogy of the ocean and the wave, which Thich Nhat Hanh speaks of, illustrates simply and beautifully the problem of this misidentification with the body. I will paraphrase. A wave will sometimes form on the surface of the ocean, exist for a time, and then disperse. The wave is, of course, made up of the same water, the same elements that make up the ocean. In essence, the wave is the ocean. Though it is a wave, a temporary ripple on the surface, it is also the ocean. If that wave were to mistake itself as being separate from the ocean, taking its temporary form to be its identity and gaining individuality, it would suffer due to the belief in its limited existence. It would suffer fear of mortality, and that fear would misshape and distort all of its perceptions and experiences, weaving its way through every aspect of its life. This is what happens to us with the belief that we are the body. The body and its consciousness are like that wave, a temporary manifestation on the surface, but consisting of the same elements as the Universal consciousness and not separate from it. When we identify ourselves with the individual body, believing we are separate from all others and the Universal, we suffer the same fear, the same anxiety as that wave. Upon dispelling that belief, the fear and all of its manifestations melt away as we gain freedom from identification with form. This is why it is so important that this misidentification be corrected. It allows us to understand that the body is nothing more than a ripple on the surface of the sea of Universal consciousness.

This answers some of the how and why as well as the question of choice, but not the question of meaning or purpose. I am aware of other people's ideas on why we take on a body: unresolved karma or unfulfilled desires from previous incarnations, or to carry on a mission or task from a previous incarnation. But these refer to reincarnation, which also stems from identification with the body. The concepts of birth, death, and rebirth pertain to the body, which is not who we are. The body is merely the vehicle for the expression of consciousness and life force as well as their food source. The likelihood of being incarnated in precisely the same way in a new body is infinitesimally small, if not entirely impossible. There is also the question of memory. As I have mentioned previously, memory is stored in the brain which dissolves with the body. Anything like wisdom that could potentially get passed on would not technically be something knowable, for in that state prior to birth, no perceiving takes place. That potential wisdom could account for the inexplicable sense of familiarity with things or for an understanding of something of which I have no prior experience. Who, though, can honestly say, when there is no way to know for sure? I can answer for certain that, upon awakening and coming to understand what awakening means, I have realized that, in breaking free from the belief that I am the body, that purpose has already begun to be fulfilled.

Then, of course, there is love. The love to be, to exist, to want to continue this existence is an aspect of consciousness. In the case of the ego, love presents as selfishness or self-centeredness, but once body identification is dropped, self-centeredness reverts to Self-love as consciousness regains its universal stature. This Self-love is love for everything and everyone as the Self encompasses all that is manifested within consciousness. What better purpose is there than that?

At this point, any remaining answers are unknown to me and frankly, they are unnecessary. I am satisfied with what I have learned, and all that has been revealed. Seeking more answers would be nothing more than an opportunity for the mind to run on a hamster wheel, expending a tremendous amount of energy but not getting anywhere. Answers to arcane questions shall, for the time being, remain unknown. I am perfectly content to leave them that way. I leave it in the hands of faith because, after all, what is faith but trusting the unknown.

A Case of
Mistaken Identity

I n the chapter titled The Unlearning Process, I discussed the major untruths that had been learned while growing up and what has been done to unlearn and replace them. Yet, there is one untruth not included in that chapter. This particular untruth's exclusion was not intentional, it was simply because my awareness and understanding had to evolve to a point where I could recognize it. This is the reason for not adding it to that chapter but speaking about it separately. To include it in the earlier chapter would interrupt the flow of the journey I have been undertaking this past year, which has unfolded in the pages of this book. This one fundamental and foundational untruth has been more detrimental and destructive than all of the others combined. In fact, all of the other untruths stem from it. I am referring to the belief that I am the body, which was discussed in the previous chapter.

As evidenced in that chapter, this mistaken belief that I am the body predates all of the other misinformation I received or that developed through my already warped perception. This belief was present in my parents, the rest of my family, and in most of society with only a few rare exceptions. The misinformation they received and the subsequent misperceptions they developed were passed down to me, helping to create the list of untruths. At the core of all of these, though, is this belief that I am the body. The belief that I am nothing more than a physical form, separate from all others, separate from the world, born and eventually going to die. This belief is the root cause of all the suffering I have endured as well as the suffering which most of society still endures today.

The belief that there was something wrong with me, which I have previously detailed, was the result of the intuitive or instinctive resistance to body identification. Unfortunately, by that point, the misidentification had already taken root. That resistance only served to strengthen the ego and the sense of separation that fuels it, thus reinforcing that destructive, negative feeling. Identification with the impermanent body creates a sense of limited life, of temporary existence sparking the fear of mortality and non-existence. That fear, coupled with the diminished nature of consciousness, brings about the feeling of being incomplete, of not being enough. From that feeling of incompleteness grows the need for fulfillment. This fulfillment is always sought outside ourselves due to our diminished nature and the subsequent misperception that fulfillment cannot come from within. The need for external fulfillment causes the distortion and perversion of love. As mentioned in the love chapter, love flows outward from within us. If we are self-seeking and self-serving, concerned only with taking, that outflow of love stops. Its polarity inverts and Self-love becomes self-centeredness. As a result, the selfless, giving nature of love becomes the need to take.

This self-centered need to take also fuels greed, and a disregard for the well-being of others, for there remains in us only selfish concern for what can be acquired. The self-centeredness and the inability to love or care about others destroy our self-esteem, leaving us feeling unworthy and undeserving of love as well. Such negativity breeds fear and mistrust of others, a feeling of separation and isolation, a sense of hostility towards the world, and it leaves us competing with others for resources for the fulfillment of our selfish desires. Addiction to drugs, alcohol, food, gambling, sex, etc., as well as the guilt, shame, remorse, and regret that accompany such destructive habits are all potentialities and pitfalls of a fear-based, selfish, self-serving lifestyle. I should include as well worry, anxiety, depression, insecurity, and whatever else the mind can conjure when guided by the self-centered, limited ego and all of its misperceptions. Then factor in improper conditioning, negative reinforcement, and harm that can come from parents, family, and society, whether intentional or accidental, which merely compound and exacerbate all that is mentioned above.

All this trouble, difficulty, and suffering arise from a simple case of mistaken identity. Okay, I admit it isn't that simple, but it is a case of mistaken identity. The body is not who we are. It is, at best, a tiny piece of who we are: a temporary manifestation in space-time like the proverbial wave on the ocean. The body is meant to be a tool, not the basis for our identity. It provides consciousness with the framework it needs because for consciousness to manifest—thus providing us with self-awareness or sentience—it requires an object to be conscious of. The body is that object. The body is also the instrument through which all of life's activities are carried out. The life force animates the body, making those activities possible. It is also the food source for said life force. We ingest food that our body converts to energy which, in turn, fuels that life force. It is also our instrument for sense perception, containing all of the sensory organs that collect data. That raw data is then interpreted by the mind and if any response is needed, the body then carries it out, and a memory of it is recorded in the brain. This is all meant to be overseen by the consciousness which is not only the observer but the experiencer as well. The body is all of these things but, as mentioned, it is not meant to be the basis for an identity, at least not beyond childhood. The ego with its body identification was not meant to be in charge much beyond adolescence. It is ill-equipped for the task of navigating adulthood with all of its complex thoughts, perceptions, feelings, emotions, responsibilities, and relationships. Through maturation and connection resulting from interactions and relationships with others, the sense of separation is meant to dissolve, in turn, dissolving the ego and its limitations due to body identification. The ego identity is meant to be outgrown. We are meant to evolve. Consciousness is meant to regain its true identity so we can live in harmony with one another, as we are all part of that consciousness. We are all waves on the same ocean: different in appearance, but one in essence. When this evolution occurs, and consciousness regains its identity, we can live free of fear and self-centeredness. We can connect and care for one another, and we can love freely and openly. Unfortunately, in our society, most do not make this evolutionary leap. Whether a result of trauma, unhealthy conditioning, broken or failed relationships or friendships, breach of trust, or a multitude of other potential factors, most remain stuck at the level of ego and its body identification. For most, there is also a lack of proper education and conditioning to make us aware of this evolutionary process. Whatever the reason for this stunted growth, all of the problems described above stem from this mistaken identity.

If we were taught all of this, the misperception of being the body would be discarded, along with the limitations, difficulties, and insecurities that accompany it. Unfortunately, this seems to be very elusive information. Coming upon such knowledge later in life as I have, while life-changing, leaves one with decades of unlearning to undertake. This assumes, of course, that one accepts such knowledge and takes it to be the truth. That in itself is a challenge because it threatens the ego's perceived existence and the very image we have of ourselves. I do not believe any of us are too keen on being unmade. Still, I would rather know than not know. Coincidentally, that need to know—that lingering feeling that something wasn't quite right, that there had to be something else, something more than this—was the driving force that led to the awakening experience and the discovery of my true nature.

Looking back with the understanding I now have, what was experienced in that awakening was freedom from the body and the illusory sense of separation that was brought about through identification with it. This separation not only created the individual ego identity but supported it as well. The light and the cleansing or purifying sensation was the light of awareness and truth washing away all of the distorted perceptions that had accumulated from this limited identity. The nurturing and care I felt was the healing nature of love I had been cut off from for so long. The witnessing of "everything" was the witnessing of consciousness and the entirety of its content, making me realize that even consciousness was not my true identity because anything perceivable cannot be me. It was witnessing from the Absolute perspective, offering a glimpse of my true nature as unmanifested awareness in which all is contained and without which none could be, existing before, behind and beyond consciousness, supporting it and the total manifestation.

What I experience now, resulting from this realization, is freedom and peace. Freedom from the misperception that I am the body and all that stems from it. Peace from the quieting of a mind that is no longer flooded with nor ravaged by fear and anxiety. The mind, ever-busy as it is, can still stir up such feelings from time to time, but I can now acknowledge them, know from whence they've come, and simply let them be. I need not respond to them. When I don't show interest or entertain them, they usually pass as quickly as they came.

I do realize that not many are going to experience the sudden, spontaneous type of awakening or realization that has happened to me. However, that does not mean that freedom is not possible. It absolutely is, so long as you can realize and accept that you are not the body: the mistaken identity that is at the root of all difficulties. Also realize that anything you can perceive is not you, that anything you perceive is merely an object in consciousness: a temporary manifestation like the body. If you can embrace these two points, then you will be well on your way, headed in the right direction. They will help loosen the grip that the ego has, as well as ease the fears and insecurities that accompany it. Begin to let go of identification with things as impermanent as the body. Instead, identify with that eternal life force that flows through you and that sense of presence that has been a constant throughout your life no matter what changes have taken place. Doing so will grant you a measure of stability and freedom that will continue to grow as other misperceptions gradually dissolve, losing their power over you in the process. Develop the habit of investigating all that your mind presents to you. See if the thoughts that arise are rooted in fear resulting from the memory of negative experiences or in anxiety about the future. If so, acknowledge that they are not rooted in present-moment reality and let them go. By all means, embrace whatever feelings arise, but also realize their fleeting nature as just another object in consciousness that is not you. Know that their foundation is not real, for past and future are not real. They only exist in the mind. This will, of course, require effort and practice. A lifetime of conditioning will not be undone overnight. However, with clear perception and identification with what is real and permanent, with persistent effort and a sincere desire to know reality and to be free of these misperceptions, it is not only possible, it is inevitable. Allow correct identification to point you in the right direction: towards your true nature, and the freedom and peace that abound from knowing your true self.

Resistance Is Futile

Have you ever stuck your hand in a river and held it against the current, attempting to stop the flow of the river? Did you succeed in doing so? Of course not. The water simply flows around your hand and on its merry way downstream. All that happens is that your hand and arm eventually become tired from resisting the current. The same is true with the flow of life. When we resist what is and what arises in the present moment, we do not stop it from occurring. We only succeed in expending unnecessary energy and wearing ourselves out. What is meant to be, will be, whether we resist it or not. Yet, we still tend to resist what is if we judge it as unpleasant or disagreeable, or if it conflicts with what we think should be.

It dawned on me that, throughout this book, I have spoken about new realizations, new insights, new information, new perceptions, and new perspectives, but I have rarely mentioned the almost inevitable resistance to these that occurs. Anything that upsets the status quo we tend to resist, even when the status quo is what has kept us trapped in false beliefs and the fear associated with them. The mind carefully constructs and seeks to reinforce these false beliefs to support the ego: the limited, individual identity. Being that the ego's essential nature is false, it requires constant reassurance to maintain its existence. It feeds off the negative energy created by the opposition and resistance toward anything that clashes with these stories, thereby upsetting the aforementioned status quo. The information presented in this book threatens the ego. It seeks to expose it as false, freeing us from its chains, which is why there will undoubtedly be resistance while reading it.

Some may resist out of sheer disbelief. To those uninitiated or untrained in spirituality and spiritual matters, as I was when I was young, this may all sound like new age, touchy-feely nonsense. This is but simple ignorance or close-mindedness, both of which can be dispelled with education and evidence. Some may have suffered trauma or abuse and have built their identity around it, mistaking who they are with what happened to them. For some, trauma or abuse is not even necessary. They build an identity around what they do: doctor, policeman, teacher, tradesman, caretaker, husband, or wife. Whatever the role, it becomes who they are. Some build an identity based on their affluence, on the riches and material possessions they amass. Resistance, in these cases, comes from the threat that the truth poses to these identities. It will expose them as false and, to those who are exposed, the fear of not knowing who they are without their identities is too overwhelming. To some, perceived uniqueness or individuality forms their identity. Dispelling the illusion of separation threatens that identity and thus, they resist. Some are obsessed with the past or future, either constantly rehashing past events in their mind or suffering anxiety about what could or might happen in the future.

They completely ignore the here and now, seeing it as nothing more than a stepping stone to the future. When confronted with the truth that past and future are but memory and anticipation, having no roots in reality and that the present moment is all that is real, they resist.

Another thing to consider regarding resistance is time, which is a very important factor. By the time we have observed what has arisen in the present moment, judged it as something we disagree with or dislike, and then attempt to resist it, that moment has already passed. What we inadvertently wind up resisting is a memory. In other words, we are resisting our minds, not actual events. The ego, of course, loves this because our attention is kept on the past, not the present moment, where the light of truth could expose its false nature. We are also focused on thoughts, not on reality. Memories are malleable, allowing for the construction of stories whereas facts are indisputable.

Please know that I am not poking at your character or trying to take anything away from you, other than misinformation and misplaced identification. I too have had my fair share of these in life and have resisted giving them up but, as the truth stripped them away, I gained a clear picture of who I am without distortions or limitations. Beneath all of the false stories and identities lies our true Self. Discovering it is truly an enlightening experience, but the process unmakes who we have believed ourselves to be. Hence, the almost inevitable resistance to anything that can bring us closer to that realization.

We are all, however, gifted with consciousness, with the awareness and presence to see all of this as it takes place. Through practice with attentiveness and self-honesty, we can learn to recognize our resistance as it arises. It often manifests as a feeling of defensiveness causing physical reactions such as tightness in the gut, chest, or shoulders. It can also present as a feeling of dislike for or the rejection of what someone has said or written. It is also generally accompanied by a desire to rationalize, justify, or explain ourselves or our position. Simple recognition and acknowledgment of our resistance are often enough to begin dispelling it. As the resistance melts away, open-mindedness and acceptance can find their way in. Then the light of truth can shine upon what would prefer to remain obscured and what is undoubtedly false so it can begin to dissolve. The truth can then begin to take root in your life, bringing about change. Freedom from misidentification and illusion, freedom from fear, and a sense of moving with the flow of life rather than against it all begin to manifest. You are then free to let the current of life take you downstream towards your ultimate destination: that wonderful discovery of your true Self.

Remember Who You Are

I feel as if our journey through these pages together is beginning to wind down. As I sit in that feeling, I contemplate what more I can share with you before I wrap things up. I am reminiscent of all that has transpired throughout the year, all that I have realized, all that I have come to understand, and all that I have shared with you thus far. So much new information has come to light and so much change has taken place, even in such a relatively short amount of time. I hope you have experienced that as well or, at the very least, that I have given you some new knowledge to contemplate and absorb. If I were to offer just one more suggestion, just one more piece of advice, it would be, as the title suggests, to always remember who you are.

Throughout these pages, I have shared with you the succession of realizations that have come to me, some of which occurred in real-time, as they were being written. These realizations have enabled me to retrace my steps, leading me back to my origin, to my true nature as unmanifested awareness. Let's review, shall we?

Initially, there was the realization of my mistaken identity as the body/mind. Freedom from that meant freedom from the ego identity and all of its distortions and limitations, which then lead to the realization of and identification as the consciousness inhabiting the body. This offered yet another measure of freedom. It gave me a "buffer zone" between me and everyday life, allowing me to still experience all that unfolded throughout the day but with a sense of detachment. This detachment keeps me from being taken over by the wave of thoughts and feelings that accompany each experience, and which cloud my perception. It allowed the clear, undistorted witnessing of all that transpires. As freeing as this was, it was still a somewhat limited scope. As the sense of separation—born of body identification and which fueled the ego—dissolved it brought about the realization of Universal consciousness which included that "body consciousness" but which extends beyond the physical form, encompassing the totality of manifestation. This was the experience of Oneness, of the connection between all things. The perception of the Self had evolved from individuality to totality and Self-love became a universal quality. It became the love for all. While this was beyond what most will experience in their lifetime, I realized that even universal consciousness had its limitations, and anything with limitations could not be the Ultimate. It was still bound by manifestation, for without manifestation there was nothing for it to be conscious of. Its attachment to manifestation is what makes consciousness perceivable and, as I've mentioned previously, anything perceivable cannot be me. I must exist prior to it to be able to perceive it, thus bringing us to the final realization as unmanifested awareness. This unmanifested "state" for lack of a better word, is a state of pure potentiality. To call it a state is technically incorrect because it presides before and beyond all states. It is entirely unbound, needing no support. It is, in fact, the support for everything else. All that manifests, everything that has come and gone comes from and returns to the Unmanifested. It is the true Source of all things. While unaware of itself, as there is nothing to be aware of, it is aware of the appearance of manifestation when it occurs. The unmanifested awareness becomes manifested consciousness for the duration of the appearance, then, as the manifestation dissolves, so does the consciousness, reverting to the unmanifested state. While I have this realization of my true nature, daily life operates and the level of consciousness being that it takes place within the manifestation. It is perceived through the lens of that temporary consciousness. The Unmanifested is the eternal, unchanging backdrop upon which all of this change, all of this living takes place. All of the aforementioned identities are me. They are merely different levels of perception, depending on the limitations at any given level. From the Absolute perspective, they are all one, just as we are all one because there is no differentiation nor separation.

This fundamental and also ultimate truth must be always remembered, for it is the foundation of a life of freedom and peace. Realizing and remembering our true Self is the key that unlocks the door to that freedom so always keep this knowledge at the forefront of your awareness. Identification with the body and the subsequent ego identity is where all suffering begins as it is the root cause of all troubles, fears, worries, insecurities, and feelings of negativity that weave their way throughout life. Remember that, as long as the body exists, the potential for identification with it exists as well and, if that happens, the ego identity will re-emerge. As mentioned in "Breaking the Habit," an old, deeply rooted pattern like this is slow to dissolve. The ego will try to latch on to events or experiences as they drift through your field of awareness by personalizing them, and it will then judge them good or bad. This will cause resistance or clinging that prevents them from passing through it as they normally would and should. The feelings and thoughts that stir up will be personalized as well, and then used to build stories about the events that give you something to mistakenly identify with and get caught up in. The ego is always trying to divert your attention from reality and the truth because it is nothing more than a false identity based on misinformation. These distractions are created to delude you and keep you in the dark. Remembering who you are is like a beacon of light shining into that darkness, illuminating it and exposing the false as false. With the truth revealed, the mind settles and becomes still and pure once it is no longer influenced by the ego and its stories. You are left dwelling in the reality of the present, with no noise and no distractions other than the occasional outside event.

This is the freedom and the peace I speak of: a quiet mind free of distractions and clear, undistorted perception, free from illusions. Life can be lived this way, though it does take practice. You need only to remember who you are. That is the only practice. You must be vigilant in your observation of the mind and its attempts to pull your attention away from reality. Whenever it tries to do so, recognize it, remember who you are, and let go of whatever false trail of breadcrumbs it is trying to lure you with. Return once again to the present moment, to reality, to the undeniable truth of who you are. Remain there as best you can, dwelling and abiding in it. Make it your home.

This is what I have learned and it is the core of my understanding, the most important thing. Everything else revolves around this remembrance. No matter what I do, where I go, who I interact with, no matter what circumstances arise in life, first and foremost, I remember who I am. I do my best to let the body/mind be. Most of what is required of it, all of the daily tasks and responsibilities, it already knows how to do and can do them automatically. I simply try to remain present in the moment aware of all that passes before me. When I do so, I create no friction, no struggle, no suffering, and can let life and all of its events and objects flow fluidly before and through me unhindered and unobstructed. "Quiet, affectionate detachment," I believe is what Maharaj used to say. When I am not caught up in the personal, I can embrace the total, the universal. Love, joy, compassion, and understanding all flow naturally when I am detached from the personal. I can treat all equally, without discrimination, because all is one. This is not only possible for you but available to you here and now. As with all I have shared in this book, I offer this knowledge to you wholly and without reservation. To take it you need only realize and then remember who you are.

Anniversary

I sit here once again, the body to be the writing instrument, to be the vessel through which these final words flow. This last chapter is more of an epilogue than a chapter because, as far as I am concerned, the book was complete with the previous chapter. I shall take this opportunity to reflect, to express overwhelming gratitude and love, and to leave you with a few parting words of thanks for having taken this journey with me.

As I sit here, it is shortly past midnight marking the anniversary of my awakening. I do realize that linear time only exists through body identification and as a function of the physical world. However, as long as there is still a body alive and existing in that world, then that time has some meaning, at least to that body, so I acknowledge this anniversary. One year ago today I awakened ... spontaneously, abruptly, unexpectedly, with nothing more than a basic understanding of spirituality and with a simple, rudimentary meditation practice. The only other help I had received up to that point was Michael Singer's book *The Untethered Soul.* From it, I had only been able to grasp that the voice in my head was not me, and that idea I had already learned through the 12-step recovery

145

process, which refers to that voice as "the disease." Beyond this, I had no other spiritual training or discipline, no teacher or guru. I had nothing more than that constant, never-satisfied feeling that there had to be something more, as well as an unyielding determination and persistence born of that feeling. Those were enough for me to awaken from my lifetime of slumber, and to shake off the dust, debris, and conditioning that left me believing I was nothing more than a body. As described in the first chapter, all of the fear and negativity I suffered as a result of that misidentification was washed away in an instant along with that identification. Given the lack of prior instruction or experience at that time, I did not understand any of this, nor did I have any idea what had just happened. The only thing I knew for sure was that some monumental shift had just occurred and that I would never be the same. That part I was right about because nothing has been the same since.

I have spent the past year researching: reading, watching videos, hearing talks, learning the language, and acquiring the information needed to understand what exactly happened that night a year ago. As evidenced throughout this book, that understanding has been acquired. However, through this process, so much more realization has occurred. I want to express gratitude for those who have awakened before me and shared their experiences, their realizations, and their understanding. They have provided me with the much-needed language and information, as well as the identification and validation that assured me I had not gone mad. Poor Kaia. I drove her crazy those first few days when I was completely overwhelmed by all of the information that was pouring out of me. I just bombarded her with it all. Thank you for being patient with me and sticking by me through that rough adjustment. I love you more than words can express.

What I have come to realize over the past year I have already detailed in other chapters, but I will sum up and bring things into the present moment. I understand my true nature, currently and temporarily as manifest consciousness, but ultimately as the unmanifested Absolute: the consciousness being the reflection of the Absolute in the cosmic mirror. This temporary, manifest consciousness is a single grain of sand in an entire beach, yet it contains within it the entire universe. All that is manifested exists within it. I understand that I am not the body nor the mind and that they are vehicles for the expression of consciousness and the life force. The life force is the energy that animates the body and is the power behind all movement and activity. Consciousness is the awareness, the sense of being or presence through which witnessing occurs. Consciousness is the seer. The life force is the doer. I understand that birth and death are merely concepts of the mind that have nothing to do with me as the Absolute, therefore there is no fear, worry, doubt, or insecurity.

Most of the time I reside in the present moment, as the present moment, witnessing all that passes before me and through me. This witnessing of life unfolding through the lens of consciousness simply happens naturally and spontaneously. All the while there is the understanding that, ultimately, it is all temporary. It is all just entertainment, not to be taken too seriously. It is merely the play of the elements and the life force, allowing consciousness to experience and love itself. I will admit that there are still occasions or intense moments that trigger strong emotions which cloud perception, allowing body identification to temporarily occur. As a result, old thought patterns re-emerge, along with the behavior that accompanies them. Those neural pathways have been carved deep over many years and are not going to go away in such a short time. However, as described in the chapter "Breaking the Habit," new, healthier patterns have been established, providing healthier choices. Regardless of how things unfold, this all belongs to the body-mind and the consciousness which experiences it. As the Absolute I take no ownership of it, I only bear witness to it through the lens of consciousness. In remembering this, these occasions are usually short-lived as they no longer have the power of the ego identity backing them. Attention is diverted only briefly before returning to the present, allowing clear perception to return, and allowing the mind to settle once again. As I grow in conviction and stabilization, solidifying the understanding of who I am, the frequency of these occurrences is diminishing.

Speaking of the mind, for the most part, it now functions as it was meant to. It works in harmony with the body interpreting sensory information, calculating, problem-solving, forming responses as needed, as well as performing its other intended functions and it does so quite well. After all, it is no longer burdened with the misinformation, stories, distorted perceptions, fears, doubts, and insecurities that accompany the limited ego identity. When the mind is not needed, its flow of thoughts recedes into the background, allowing the stillness and alertness of presence to fill the foreground, keeping my attention in the here and now. The incessant, never-ending chatter that was always so distracting has subsided. If this were the only benefit I had received from all this, it would have been enough.

The flame in the heart remains, ever-present. When fanned by a mere half-smile it grows to a roaring fire that burns away any negativity that tries to creep back in. Love—the warm, healing energy that courses throughout the body—is still constantly flowing outward. Like consciousness, that love has been freed from false identification and distortion and is no longer limited. It is the love of the Self, bearing in mind that the Self is universal, not individual. It is a love that is completely selfless, all-encompassing, and all-embracing. It is this all-encompassing love that connects us, creating the sense of Oneness. The illusion of separation is no more.

At this point, there is nothing for me to do. Not that there ever was, as doing is a function of the body, animated by the life force. The only thing to "do" is to simply be, without being this or that. Simply live free of false identification and attachment, aware of the witnessing that spontaneously takes place. For the time being, as I am still stabilizing. I also try to be aware of the reactions and responses of the body-mind to determine if there are any lingering remnants of the false self. In other words, if those reactions and responses are old, familiar feelings or thoughts related to past experiences rather than to the current situation, or are perhaps worry-based, rooted in some imagined future, I dismiss them and let them go. I do, of course, acknowledge whatever feelings arise, but I also realize that the foundation for them, whatever spawned them, is false. Beyond this, the only task is to grow in conviction. The hope is that the Absolute "state" becomes the constant, and the temporary sentient state is viewed merely as an occurrence or appearance. Consciousness will then be perceived as an instrument of the Absolute, providing the vehicle for experiencing, in the same way that the mind and body provide the vehicles for thought and action. I realize that for this to occur before the "death" of the body is extremely rare. Relinquishing the identity as consciousness is as difficult as relinquishing the ego identity while the body still exists. I know it is possible though because it has happened to others, and I have also been given glimpses of it in that initial awakening as well as in meditation. After all, it is my natural, eternal state. Until then, I will abide in consciousness. Freedom from body identification and the ego is already more than I could have ever hoped for or even imagined. Also, to finally satiate and satisfy that lifelong feeling that there has to be something more, to finally be free of that; words cannot adequately express that sense of relief. The ones that come close are overwhelming gratitude and appreciation.

Finally, to you, the reader, my friend, I say thank you once again. Thank you for taking the time to read this book. Thank you for taking this journey with me. To you, I humbly express gratitude and love. I hope that something in these pages gave you satisfaction and joy, perhaps even identification, education, and clarification. I hope that something in these pages has planted a seed in you that will grow to fruition and become your awakening if that has not already happened. It may feel as if this journey has come to an end, but rest assured, this is only the beginning.

Edit/Update: As there have been revisions to the rest of the chapters that reflect the deeper understanding, it only seems fair that I update this epilogue as well and let you know that it has all come to pass.

The Absolute or Unmanifested is now clearly seen as the point of origin, our true nature as the title suggests. It is also the constant, eternal backdrop upon which or within which all transient appearance happens. The consciousness, the current, temporary nature is both the instrument through which witnessing takes place as well as the proof of that original state. There was no awareness of myself as an entity in the Unmanifested, as it is a state of pure potentiality, devoid of manifestation. Therefore, the apparatus for witnessing, for sentience, did not exist. However, for me to be able to currently say "I am conscious," there had to be existence before consciousness to provide a point of contrast to the current state in which the uttering of those words is possible. In other words, I had to "be" before the appearance of consciousness to know that I am now conscious. As mentioned previously, anything perceivable cannot be me. I must exist before it to be able to perceive it and this conscious state, this sentience, is indeed perceivable.

Conviction has grown to the point where there is no doubt that what was just expressed is true. Stabilization has improved to the point where any disturbances that occur in daily life, any remnants of ego and body identification that may surface, are viewed as mere movements in consciousness, simply objects of the witnessing that is constantly happening. Such disturbances are recognized as false and promptly dismissed. Any feelings or thoughts accompanying these occurrences are also just movements in consciousness that are witnessed. They are all seen as nothing more than temporary appearances.

Stillness has become the natural state. Movements, events, occurrences, activities, feelings, and thoughts all appear for a time and then disappear upon that background of stillness in the same way that sounds appear and then disappear upon the background of silence. Stillness, like silence, has become the constant that presides before, after, in between, and as the backdrop behind all of these temporary appearances in consciousness.

Beyond this, there is nothing more to say, nothing more that can be said, as words do not reach beyond the limitations of consciousness. The best they can do is point the way towards our true nature. The rest happens spontaneously because, without the ego identity, there is no "doer" to take the supposed journey. The rest is just the realization of the timeless truth of what we are. With that realization, I recede into and remain in stillness and silence.

Printed in the United States
by Baker & Taylor Publisher Services

Printed in the United States
by Baker & Taylor Publisher Services